My
Seasons

A literary celebration of sports and life

BOB WELCH

AO CREATIVE
Eugene, Oregon

Publisher's note: Many of the stories in this book originally appeared in *Stories from the Game of Life,* published by Harvest House Publishers, Eugene, Oregon, in 2000. The rights have been purchased by the author.

Published by AO CREATIVE
P.O. Box 41794
Eugene, Oregon 97404
www.aocreative.com

Front cover: The author (Oregon Duck shirt) with fellow Turkey Bowl participants — and two fans — prior to the 1973 game at Cloverland Park in Corvallis, Oregon. Standing, left to right: Fans Janet Corcoran Wright and Jay Locey. Players Tom Boubel, John Mills and Craig Morris. Kneeling: Dan Roberts, John Woodman, Steve Scholl and Brad Hoffman. On book's spine: Lee Jacobson. (Warren Welch photo)

Back cover photo by Sally Welch

ISBN: 0-9772306-1-9

Printed in Canada

Author information:
www.bobwelch.net
info@bobwelch.net

Also by Bob Welch

My Oregon
American Nightingale
The Things That Matter Most
Stories from the Game of Life
Where Roots Grow Deep
A Father for All Seasons
More to Life Than Having It All
Bellevue and the New East Side

To my mother, Marolyn,
who's never stopped cheering for me —
or challenging herself.

Table of contents

The greatest glory of sport is that it teaches us so much about life itself.

— Ahmad Rashad

Introduction

I am turning some friends' sprawling country lawn into a field of dreams for our traditional Independence Day Wiffle Ball Game.

Three 5-gallon buckets of lime await. The lime will be poured into the metal pouch of my new Alumagoal All-Steel Dry Line Marker, a two-wheeled beauty that I ordered from back East.

Guided by a 100-foot tape measure, I will mark a pair of 4-inch white lines: the third-base line stretching north, almost to the barn in left, the first-base line stretching east to the wire fence in right.

After the barbecue dinner, in keeping with tradition, all players — some no taller than a baseball bat — will line up next to the third-base line, but not on it, lest they incur the wrath of a certain proud groundskeeper. And accompanied by a CD, we will sing *The Star-Spangled Banner.*

You see, it just won't go away.

I'm 52, old enough to know better. But in an array of ways, my love for sports abides like those two chalked lines will not. A few mowings and sprinklings and those lines will fade, almost as if they never existed. But my soul seems, well, permanently chalked.

This sports thing is etched so deeply in me that, as readers of my general column in the newspaper occasionally remind me, when I go searching for a metaphor I almost always find it in a ball park.

I've seen sports from nearly every perspective imaginable: as a player, referee, coach, sportswriter, father, fan — and, yep, even as a concessionaire, having sold popcorn and Cracker Jacks for a summer of seemingly endless American Legion baseball.

I've interviewed, in person, such athletes as Arnold Palmer, Peter Jacobsen and Alberto Salazar, at one time the greatest marathon runner in the world. I've eaten breakfast with the late author and Walter-Mitty-of-sports George Plimpton and lunched with Olympic gold medalist Dick Fosbury. I've covered Final Four basketball tournaments, played Pebble Beach twice, run two marathons, written stories from the Orange Bowl press box and been published in *Sports Illustrated*. I saw Ken Griffey Jr. hit his first major-league home run and saw the late Steve Prefontaine run his final race, only hours before his death.

And yet what intrigues me most about sports has less to do with famous athletes than with the fascination of athletes of all abilities creating something from nothing; less to do with get-rich contracts than with deep-down character; less to do with the headlines than with the heart. In particular, I'm intrigued by sports as a microcosm of life itself, the ebbs and flows of, say, a basketball game mirroring the ebbs and flows of our day-to-day existence.

Sports is a canvas on which athletes, as artists, create new works each day, no two alike.

It's a classroom in which the lessons of life are learned.

It's a meeting place in which people draw near to one another, sometimes by identifying with a hero or team; sometimes by learning the value of teamwork; sometimes by realizing, as do some fathers and sons, that sports is one of the few things the two might have in common — not an end in itself, necessarily, but a means to an end, an entry to a deeper place.

Some people think of sports and think of some Joe Six Pack with a remote surgically affixed to his hand. That's not me. I can't name a dozen current major league baseball players. I seldom watch a complete NFL game on TV. And I wouldn't miss the NBA if players were to go on permanent strike because, as Latrell Spreewell said while moaning about his then-$14.6 million contract, "I've got to feed my family."

My love for sports has always been rooted in more soulful soils:

the beauty of a baseball stadium as early evening shadows descend, the undying spirit of an underdog and the way an allegiance to a team draws disparate people together like the fires at my late-autumn football tailgaters.

While in Orlando, Florida, for a book publishing convention, I noted guests who hurriedly came and went, lost in their own little worlds, seemingly oblivious to one another. But when the U.S. women's soccer team began its quest to beat China in the World Cup championships, people began gathering around the lobby TV like moths to a flame. Soon, these strangers were cheering with one another, commiserating with one another, connecting with one another with an almost-instantaneous sense of oneness.

Sports does that. I can't tell you how much money my late father made per year or how much our carpet cost per foot. But 40 years later, I can still remember playing knee football with that man on the living room rug on Sunday nights after *Lassie*.

I can't remember whether our first car was a V-6 or a V-8, but I remember the day Sally, then my wife of two years, subbed for the youth baseball team I coached. I remember the snickers when she stepped to the plate, the sudden quiet when she ripped a double to right-center and the pitcher softly saying "Wow."

I can't remember a single purchase I made in the year 1995, but I remember, with great clarity, the way the sun broke through the early morning haze as my son Ryan and I golfed our way down the Oregon Coast on a 7-mile-long hole we'd created.

Not that sports is sanctified with some sort of innate goodness or is superior to music or art or anything else as a way of infusing our lives with meaning. Witness Tour de France winner Floyd Landis blood-doping, soccer fans rioting and tee-ball parents acting less mature than the 5-year-olds on the field. Still, sports remains one of the arenas in which lives are shaped, courage is tested, faith is steeled. In an ever-changing world, it's a place of permanence; the national anthem is always sung before a game, stilling your soul for just a few moments that border on the sacred.

It's a place rooted deep in America. The poet Robert Frost may be best remembered for two paths diverging into the wood and horses stopping by woods on snowy eves, but a sportswriter for his high school paper in New Hampshire lauded him for his play at defensive end. "No one would think the man who played football on the right end was the same person who sits with spectacles astride his nose in the Chief Editor's Chair. Keep up the good work, Bobby!"

It's a place where tradition is still revered; at a Seattle-area paper where I once worked, the publisher would walk into the newsroom one day each April and throw out the "opening pitch" of the major league baseball season.

It's a place laced with earthy ambiance; a withered hot dog that might make you nauseous if eaten at a convenience store would, if eaten at a baseball stadium, taste stunning.

It's a place that marks the passage of time.

When I smell Oregon's late-summer field burning, I'm reminded that football will soon start. Come November, when Oregon's infamous rains begin clogging gutters, I'm reminded that basketball will soon start. When I smell the first cut grass of the year, usually late February, I'm reminded that baseball will soon start.

This book, I suppose, is an attempt to define not only such literal seasons, but also the more ethereal seasons. The seasons of my life. And, if I've done my job right, the seasons of *your* lives, unlocked by the stories that follow.

Many of these stories were originally published in a book I wrote called *Stories of the Game of Life* (2000) that's out of print. A few stories have been culled from other books I've written. And a dozen pieces are fresh out of the oven, which isn't meant to suggest that they're half-baked, only that I do occasionally offer a non-sports metaphor.

Together, they comprise my attempt to celebrate the twining of sports and life. To reach beyond the game that most people see. And to explain, without apology, why a 52-year-old man can look at two white lines on a swath of green grass and feel the joy of being 12 years old again.

Bob Welch
Eugene, Oregon
September 2006

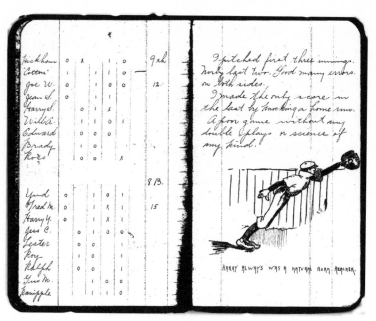

From the 1905 sandlot baseball journal of Will Adams, the author's grandfather. "Harry always was a natural born reacher." See Page 204.

Weary the years that have passed since then,
Who dreamed as the star dust fluttered down
Of fame that fluttered beyond the years,
Of glory hooked to the sweep of cheers,
A kid who looked to the heights some day,
Over the hills and far away ...
— Grantland Rice

1
The
Game

Welch Turkey Bowl 1986: Ryan revels smugly in victory while Sally consoles Jason, deep in the agony of defeat. (Bob Welch)

Field of dreams

I was doing some garage-sale pricing, going through all that leftover stuff of life that my wife, Sally, and I were only too glad to sell to someone else, when I came upon it: a little Atlanta Braves hat that looked decidedly small, as if it could fit on one of those bobblehead dolls you used to see in the rear windows of cars.

"Whatayathink, twenty-five cents?" she asked.

I barely heard her. Because when I saw that hat, I was back in the early '90s, in our backyard, firing a Wiffle ball to a 10-year-old son wearing that hat, a kid whose nickname was Rosebud because, like Ted Williams, he had a tendency to yank everything down the right-field line, the foul territory of which consisted of his mother's rose bushes.

Now when I say right-field line you need to visualize a left-field line because — well, because like most neighborhood baseball leagues, the Backyard Baseball Association (BBA) was not exactly conventional.

The league was founded in the early '90s, the creation of my two sons, 11 and 8 at the time, and a couple of their pals of similar ages. Among their first decisions was that first base would be located at what we traditionally think of as third base. Why? Because our rectangular backyard — not much bigger than a doubles tennis court — was situated in such a way that if you were to overrun first base in its traditional location, you would smash into the right field fence, which was only about five feet beyond the bag.

(Over the years, this reverse-direction motif worked well, the only hitch coming after Michael Jenson, one of Jason's pals and a kid on my Kidsports baseball team, once spent the night. The boys played BBA for about four hours that evening. The next morning, in a Kidsports game, Michael stepped to the plate, drove a single through the infield and promptly raced for third base. Fortunately, with me screaming from the third-base coach's box, he turned from his wayward ways and safely reached first.)

So you get the idea: The (traditional) right field fence was shallow, a mere 30 feet from home plate. The (traditional) left field fence was 51 feet down the line, homers landing in Bendix Street and beyond.

Given such dimensions, you might assume that right field was the poke of preference. But a mere five feet from the right field fence was the garage of Mr. West, who spent nearly every waking hour working in that garage. Mr. West was a nice man; if he'd had a nickel for every Wiffle or tennis ball he tossed back in our yard during the nearly decade-long BBA existence, he could have bought the Yankees and had change to acquire Mike Piazza from the Mets.

But the BBA had a you-hit-it/you-get-it rule and nobody liked the hassle of climbing the fence and facing Mr. West. What also made right field a risky choice was that every obstacle around the field was live, meaning that a ball on Mr. West's slanted garage roof could, and sometimes would, bounce back into right field for an out.

Center field, 59 feet from the plate, was an all-but-impossible shot because a towering Douglas fir stood just beyond the pitcher's mound not only took away dead center, but the power alleys as well. That, of course, meant (traditional) left field was homer heaven, which always rankled young Jared McDonald, a left-handed hitter who had to go opposite field for his tators and still has about half a dozen would-be homers stuck in the bad-news branches of that tree.

Jesse, his younger brother, was a streak hitter, a kid whose first love was skate boarding and whose commitment to the game was forever being questioned by the press.

Jason, my younger son, was the smallest of the four, the foul ball king. He would rip three or four fall balls into the rose bushes or onto our house's deck — we were continually restringing the wind chimes his great-grandfather, "Pop," made us — and then hit a double or triple down the line.

Ryan, my older son, was the leader. He made the rules. ("If your team is ahead by 6, you have to bat opposite handed ... No arguing ... No changing rules during games, unless everyone agrees ...").

He edited the *BBA News*, a computer-generated weekly. ("The Bendix Buddies team is without lead-off hitter Jesse McDonald because of contract complications ... The second game of the doubleheader was cut short because it was past Jared's bedtime ... The Bendix Buddies are having trouble keeping reporters out of the clubhouse ... .")

He drew up the contracts. ("I —— make a commitment to play on the Bendix Buddies baseball team. And to play to the best of my ability in every game. I promise to miss only —— practices and only —— games. If I happen to miss more of either I agree to be dealt a one-game suspension.")

He kept the statistics. ("Welch went 15-for-18 with four doubles, 14 RBIs, five home runs, and a grand slam, including two Effie Balls, one in the third deck.")

The ultimate hit was what the boys called an "Effie Ball," named in honor of Effie, the widow who lived across Bendix Street from the left-field fence, a woman who seemed to consider Wiffle balls in her rhododendrons more of an honor than an annoyance. Hitting Effie's duplex meant a blow of at least 100 feet, 120 to the second deck (the porch area above her garage) and 130 feet to the third and upper deck (her roof).

Games were usually two-on-two, often Ryan and Jared vs. the two younger boys. Sometimes, I was called to be "all-time pitcher" to both teams. On such occasions, I would, in the spirit of professional wrestling, create different personas for myself, including "Robo Pitcher," whose over-the-top jerky motion was always met with a barrage of boos, and the ever-controversial "Sidearm Sammy," a closer from the South who threw such a wicked sidearm pitch that he jokingly claimed he actually released the ball from a neighboring zip-code area.

Whatever moundsmen my mind could conceive, their common denominator was this: All got unmercifully shelled. You might say I had a multiple personality pitching disorder. I can still hear the hoots and hollers as I'd slink to the garden shed, i.e., "the showers," having once again been yanked by my impatient manager. And yet in the never-say-die spirit of sports, I would soon emerge — fist pumping in the air while the p.a. announcer introduced me — as some New Hope, the arm destined to bring this cocky kiddy corps to their humble knees.

Then one of the kids would do something like bounce a line drive off my forehead and it was back to the garden shed, the laughter from my opponents following me like pesky mosquitoes.

Like all good backyard leagues, what made BBA work was, as Yogi Berra might have said, 75 percent physical and the other half imagination. The boys would emerge from the house wearing the strangest uniforms imaginable — not some color-coordinated motif that came neatly folded in a box from Toys R Us, but wild stuff: multiple sweat bands, masking-taped numbers, batters' shin guards made from old football thigh pads, perhaps an ankle wrap to give them that "I'm-hurt-but-still-tough-enough-to-play" look.

We built a chicken-wire backstop and a plywood scoreboard — "Welch Stadium" it said — whose Home and Visitors numbers were changed by spinning four wooden dials about the sizes of large pizzas. We used old poker chips to designate balls, strikes and outs.

The garden shed-turned-clubhouse was stocked with all sorts of bats — plastic, wood, re-tooled broomsticks, duct-tape enhanced, you name it — and other stuff: catcher's gear, Kool-Aid, cups, a chalkboard, and a never-ending supply of sunflower seeds. Night games were lit with a halogen floodlight positioned atop the shed.

We used mainly Wiffle balls until they inevitably cracked, then we fortified them with duct tape, sometimes after wrapping them in yarn so every ball wouldn't be an Effie Ball.

Videos were sometimes taken from a camera positioned on our almost-flat back porch roof. A taped version of *The Star-Spangled Banner* would begin special games, including one World Series in which we invited Jared and Jesse's parents over for grilled hot dogs and the game.

Occasionally, All-Star games would be played, an interesting concept because traditionally such games feature only the league's best players, but I never remember any of the four BBA players NOT making the team. I do remember some suspensions, however; like life itself, BBA was not without its darker side. As I recall, most suspensions involved the younger two players not taking the game as seriously as the older two thought necessary.

I remember a few thousand "out-safe" controversies — a batter was out if he didn't reach second base before the ball was thrown against the side of the house — and, of course, the controversial Deck Addition of '95, in which the Adult Housing Authority allegedly ramrodded through a proposal to shave off a smidge of the field as part of a kitchen add-on project.

"Smidge? You gotta be joking," said Ryan, the BBA's union representative, whose defiance suggested the AHA's proposal was like someone recommending taking off just a smidge of Mona Lisa's smile.

The AHA won that battle and, in later years, was able to put a small apple tree in foul territory down the (traditional) third baseline. When BBA gave way in the mid-'90s to teenagers with cars and jobs and arms so strong that Effie's duplex would have been Wiffled to smithereens, a maple tree went into shallow (traditional) right.

Like an Ebbets Field relic, the scoreboard now lies on the side of the house, the victim of a decade of Oregon rain and a designer who stupidly chose interior plywood. Effie moved to Idaho and later died. The boys of summer have become men.

"Hello, Earth to Bob," said Sally, waking me from the past. "So, twenty-five cents for the hat?"

We sold a ton of stuff at the garage sale on that Saturday morning not long ago. We sold a refrigerator, exercycle, hundreds of golf balls and a camp saw so cheaply made you'd have thought it came in a Cracker Jack box. We even sold a bunch of hats for a quarter a piece.

But Jason's Atlanta Braves hat never made it to the display floor. It now hangs proudly near my workbench, alongside one of his brother's. They are gentle reminders of the way it was on summer nights when little boys would slap a Wiffle ball into the sky and, with faces flushed with big-league determination, race madly for third base.

Wings to fly

It has sat vacant in my old hometown for more than a decade now: store space once home to Les & Bob's Sporting Goods. Now, whenever I drive by it on Fourth Street in downtown Corvallis, the memories are unleashed as if I've just caught a whiff of campfire smoke and am suddenly camping as a child.

Memories not only about the store, but about this community that nurtured the store. About the early '60s, a time so innocent that your life's biggest concern seemed to be getting tagged out while playing hot box with the Larkin brothers. About a boyhood spent on ball fields and in Friday-night gymnasiums that smelled of popcorn and on the cross-country trails of Avery Park.

Once, after the "Out of Business" sign had been slapped up, I pulled over and peered through the dirty windows.

The oil and leather smell of "The Claw," a baseball mitt I bought for $15 when I was 12 ... the sound of baseball cards in the spokes of my 24-inch Schwinn ... Playing one-on-one football in front of Garfield School with Robbie Younger in the rain ... .

Les & Bob's was not where childhood dreams were born or played out. Instead, it was where dreams were given wings to fly — wings that came in size 3 Chuck Taylor Converse All-Star basketball shoes and Wilson "Ed-U-Cated" heel baseball gloves and little silver needles through which air could inflate a flattened basketball and a young boy's imagination.

In the 1960s, Les & Bob's was to the kids in my town what a general store in Springfield, Missouri, was to the people who came West on the wagon trains a century earlier — a place to get equipped for journeys to The Promised Land. Those journeys often turned out to be more promising in the minds of those taking them than in real life, which is perhaps why the place I got equipped still holds such fond memories: It was a place yet untarnished by life's inevitable defeats.

> *The sound of a brand-new bat hitting a new ball as I singled to center in the Midget League All-Star game ... secretly listening to my transistor radio in Mr. Brown's fourth-grade class at Garfield School as Sandy Koufax and the Dodgers beat the Yankees four straight in the '63 Series ... while home "sick" — and my folks gone — high-jumping onto my bed, pretending I was Oregon State's Dick Fosbury ... .*

Unlike now, when you're not apt to find Mr. Goodwrench checking your car's timing belt or Wendy cooking your burger, when you walked into a sporting goods store named Les & Bob's in 1965, it was owned and operated by a guy named Les and a guy named Bob. One of them, Bob I think, wore lots of shaving lotion; he could be helping a kid in the barbells section and you could smell him from the baseball section. The two of them knew virtually every kid who had ever played sports at Corvallis High School; even if you were a so-so athlete like me, they made you feel like an MVP.

If you lived in Corvallis in the '50s and '60s and bought a baseball glove or football pants or catcher's mask, you bought it at Les & Bob's. Today, you can get such items at just about any one-stop-shopping store in Corvallis. And you can get way more than Les & Bob's offered.

In the early '60s, the only type of sweatsuit you could buy was the baggy gray kind. You couldn't buy sweatbands because they hadn't been invented yet. Nor could you buy the multitude of hats and shirts emblazened with logos of professional and college teams.

But even though, by today's standards, the choices at Les & Bob's were limited, I never felt that way then. I felt like when I walked in that store, anything was possible.

Playing hockey in Mark Baker's living room, using his dad's putter and a three-iron for sticks ... building a scale model of Dodger Stadium out of balsa wood ... staying after Mr. Sprick's social studies class at Cheldelin Junior High to play "finger-kick football" in which we'd draw a goalpost on the chalkboard, make these triangular "footballs" out of notebook paper and, using the flick of a finger, "kick" field goals. (Mr. Sprick, whose life in a wheelchair had left him with powerful arms and fingers, was our hero. He not only knew U.S. history but could nail kicks from the back row with regularity.)

In the Les & Bob's sanctuary of sports, the ultimate chapel of dreams was a tiny nook in the back right corner: an area no larger than a small bedroom, lined floor to ceiling on three sides with shoes. It had a vinyl sofa, where you sat to be fitted.

To buy your first pair of Chuck Taylor Converse All-Star shoes at Les & Bob's was to engage in a rite of passage that seemed almost as hallowed as anything that might happen at church. The room had a smell like no other place: the smell of Chuck Taylor Converse All-Star rubber. The smell of newness. Of new seasons. Of beginnings.

You could buy a handful of specialty shoes at Les & Bob's — I still remember my royal blue Adidas Tokyo track shoes — but mainly what you could buy were Converse. And your choice of Converse was simple: black low-tops, black high-tops, white low-tops and white high-tops.

When you laced up a pair of Converse Chuck Taylor All-Star's and realized they fit and your mother was standing nearby with the $8 to buy them, you felt you'd been given wings to fly. You felt like Billy Bam, the kid in the old Nestle's Quik commercials who, after gulping down a glass of chocolate milk, could play basketball at warp speed, scoring at will.

... Playing basketball on Sunday afternoons in Oregon State's Gill Coliseum, where Louisiana State's legendary "Pistol" Pete Maravich had once played a game, the only difference being Pete didn't have to worry about a janitor kicking him and his pals out ... At 11, winning a football autographed by Oregon State's football team for the "Beaver Huddle Armchair Quarterback Contest," meaning I was the entrant closest to predicting the score of the Oregon State-Syracuse football game. And after vowing to never take that football off my shelf, using it for a game of street football within a week, the names so badly scuffed you couldn't read them if you'd been Inspector Clouseau himself.

Near as I can tell, I made the first trip to Les & Bob's when I was 8. I know this because I have, in an old scrapbook, the following letter, whose spelling and punctuation I've left in their original state — the literary equivalent of a box score forever preserved with embarrassing errors: "To My Mom. I'm glad your my mother because your sweet and kind and you let me go places like May 10th you took me to Less and Bob to get a baseball hat and you ironed the letters OSU on it. I like you because your leting me go out for little leaghg baseball. Love, Bobby."

Listening to an Oregon State football game on the radio at my grand-father's beach cabin, Bob Blackburn's voice fading in and out, a thrilling touchdown run sometimes interrupted by a commercial for Ron Tonkin Chevrolet in Portland or a weather report from Salt Lake City or marimba music from Mexico ... Playing night football in a foot of snow at OSU's Parker Stadium ... Riding my bicycle five miles across town to Marysville Golf Course, my plaid bag of clubs on my shoulder ... .

In 1963, you could buy one style of kids' football pants at Les & Bob's — cheesy red pants with cardboard thigh pads. I wanted them desperately. If I got those pants, I figured, I could someday be Heisman Trophy winner Terry Baker, the Oregon State quarterback who, in 1962, won the Liberty Bowl with a 99-yard touchdown run.

"Youre the best Mother in the world," I wrote my mother in my grammar-impaired English, the rest of the sentence looking like the remains of an Amtrak wreck. "Mother it is why you are going to buy that football sut with pads. thingk you."

Playing an entire Far West Classic basketball tournament in my drive-way with just me, an orange-covered scorebook I'd gotten for Christmas, and my imagination ... The smell of the Willamette Valley's grass seed fields being burned in late August and realizing no matter how sickening the thought of school starting and me once again not getting the 64-Cray-on box like some other kids undoubtedly would get, all was well with the world because the smell of that smoke meant football was almost here ... Looking at the cleat marks in the mud of Spartan Field on foggy Saturday mornings and thinking with awe that, just the night before, I'd seen the very players who made those cleat marks.

Once, when my younger son, Jason, was 17, my wife and I were with him at a huge chain sporting goods store in which one entire floor was devoted strictly to shoes. While Jason browsed for shoes, I started counting the number of different styles available because I was amazed at the selection.

I counted three hundred and forty-seven different kinds. I was thinking about the little shoe room at Les & Bob's and how it probably had a dozen different styles at most.

My sons grew up in a world far different from the one I did. They laugh at my stories of Les & Bob's shoe room, about plain gray sweatpants, about how few choices I had when I was growing up.

But, then, maybe that's what made my boyhood seem so strangely blessed, made the seemingly simple seem so profound, made what little we had seem so very, very big.

The reasons why

Jason was a seventh-grader playing in an eighth-grade baseball league. More than that, on this particular day he was a sapling in a forest of towering firs. The team I was coaching — and he was playing shortstop for — was down 4-zip to a team from the foothills of the Cascade Mountains, a bunch of country boys who looked as if their fathers were lumberjacks. The pitcher was more than a foot taller than my 4-foot-9-inch son and had a catapult for an arm.

From my third-base coach's box, I mentally gulped when Jason dug into the batter's box.

The pitcher's first pitch was a fast ball that Jason appeared to have noticed only when he heard it smack in the catcher's glove, sounding like the thud of a fireworks rocketing into the sky. The second pitch scorched the plate for a called strike two.

The third pitch came right at Jason. He turned to avoid being hit and fell to the ground. His bat went flying. His helmet bounced off. The ball seemed to have skimmed his shoulder.

"Take your base," said the umpire.

Standing in the third-base coach's box, I was happy just seeing Jason alive, much less getting a free base out of the deal. But, oddly, I noticed him saying something to the umpire. What was going on?

"It didn't hit me," Jason said.

"Take your base, son," said the ump. "It did."

Our fans were likely thinking the same thing I was thinking: *Take your base. You've been wounded, soldier; your war's over. You're going home ....*

"But, honest, it didn't hit me," Jason pleaded.

The umpire looked at Jason and out to the infield ump, who responded with a "whatever" shrug. "OK," said the home-plate ump. "The count is one and two."

Should I intervene? Make him take his base? Argue for the free ticket to first?

Jason was already back in the batter's box, looking back at the pitcher, taking his practice swings. I shrugged and headed back to the coach's box.

The towering pitcher rocked and fired a bullet right down the middle, the kind of pitch that would send the kid to the dugout.

Jason ripped it into left-center field for a standup double.

Our crowd roared. I just stood there, looking at the kid standing on second, unstrapping his batting glove. The manager of the opposing team was standing a few feet behind me. He spit out his sunflower seeds and slowly shook his head.

"Man," he said. "Ya gotta love that."

He had no idea the kid was my son. But that didn't matter. In fact, it made the comment all the sweeter.

Why do sports have such a hold on us? Why do we love this stuff? In part, because of moments like these. Because of the game itself. Because you never know what will happen.

Music and theater draw us for other reasons, little of which has to do with the unexpected. Without opposition, there's little room to stray from the script.

But there's opposition in sports. And no script. Every moment is susceptible to the unexpected. To chance. To the awkward bounce of a fumbled football, the sudden gust of wind on a golf course, the routine grounder to second base that 99 times out of 100 times will be fielded and thrown easily to first base but one time — one time — is not.

Oregon State is tied with North Carolina 2-all in the eighth inning of the deciding game for the NCAA baseball championships in June 2006 with runners at first and second base and two outs. OSU's Ryan

Gipson grounds to second. Routine out, end of inning, right?

Wrong. Instead, the North Carolina second baseman throws wide, a run scores and Oregon State — a rain-forest team in a sun-splashed sport — wins the championship, the first truly northern team to win since Ohio State in 1966. Having won six do-or-die games in the process, the Beavers complete what may have been the most stunning college baseball story in history — in part because of the one-in-a-hundred throw.

So, yes, because of the game itself. But also because of the anticipation before and during that game.

It's late August and you arrive home from work to find a thick envelope — your season football tickets. Yes!

You watch your 5-iron shot soar toward a green and there's this frozen time in which you measure the ball against its target. Is it enough? Too much? Will it bite? Roll?

You watch a quarterback unleash a bomb to a receiver being shadowed stride for stride by a defensive back. Is it enough? Too much? Can he catch it? Can the defender bat it down?

It's these seconds that comprise a play, a game and, ultimately, a season. So, yes, we love sports because of the anticipation. But also because of the game within a game. The thinking that's going on at field level that's not always discerned at fan level: a hit-and-run play at the right moment, a defensive blitz at the right moment, a stolen basketball pass at the right moment.

Sometimes the "game within a game" manifests itself in some new-fangled sports technique, as Oregon State's Dick Fosbury proved in 1963. The Medford High high-jumper learned he could soar higher by flipping over the bar backward rather than using the traditional "western roll." People laughed. Five years later, though, he stood on the Olympic gold medal podium in Mexico City as the best high-jumper on the planet. And now, the "Fosbury Flop" is virtually the only technique used.

So, yes, because of the game within a game. But also because of the game *beyond* the game: The people who make up the game. The players, coaches, managers, umpires, fans, peanut vendors, owners. The woman who sings the national anthem. The kids down the foul lines scooping grounders. The father who taught the kid on the mound how to grip a baseball. The mother who refused to give up on a son who wanted to give up on himself.

In Steve Kettmann's *One Day at Fenway*, he takes a single baseball game and shows us the myriad influences on that game, including the Red Sox groundskeeping crew. "(They) had more influence over the bounce of a ball than people knew. If a sinkerballer like Derek Lowe was pitching for the Red Sox, they would leave the infield grass unmowed for a day to help keep down all those grounders off the bats of opposing hitters. The ball would zig or zag more or less depending on which type of grass they used."

Surrounding that field, fans have an influence, too. Sometimes that influence is quirky — say, the guy who leans over the railing and, by catching the ball, robs an outfielder of a chance to do the same. Or as I witnessed in Miami in the 1985 Orange Bowl, Oklahoma's "Sooner Schooner" rolling onto the field after a successful field goal against Washington — only to incur a delay-of-game penalty and forcing a re-kick that missed. End of Oklahoma rally. Washington goes on to win.

I've seen games at University of Oregon's McArthur Court, the second-oldest college basketball venue in America, where I believe a wild crowd in the Cracker-Jack-box gym gave the home-team Ducks a 10-point advantage.

Fans make a difference. In football, when the UO's defense is in a third-down situation, I'm convinced that the louder our crowd, the less chance the opposing team will have of making a first down. I know it borders on the neurotic, but I'm also semi-convinced that the more closely connected I am to a UO game, the better chance we have to win. Being there, of course, is the ultimate connection, followed by watching on TV and listening on radio. Watching a taped-delay is dangerous — I hate that feeling that the outcome has already been decided and no energy of mine can change it. And being out of the country is the absolute worst. Once, I left for Haiti with Oregon 6-1 and contending for a Rose Bowl berth. On the day I landed in Port au Prince, our starting quarterback was knocked out of the game, we lost three of what would be five straight games and wound up with no bowl bid at all. And it was all my fault.

So, yes, we love sports because of the people who make up the game — from athlete to fan to groundskeeper. But also because of the venues, the places where these games are played. Places that influence the experience.

In 1967, as a 13-year-old Beaver fan, I watched Oregon State's "Giant Killers" upset No. 1 ranked USC 3-0 in rainy Corvallis, in part because O.J. Simpson could never get untracked in Parker Stadium's mud. The field clearly made a difference in the game.

Domes, of course, have robbed sports of many such variables, neutering the venue into the role of impotent onlooker, fields becoming as boringly similar as bowling lanes.

But beyond these icons of antiseptic sameness, sports venues have their say. Golf courses offer variables galore; depending on their nature, they can work against, say, a player who fades the ball or a long-ball hitter or a guy who turns to jelly on super-undulating greens. Beyond influencing outcomes, venues influence us. The fan. And our experience.

Like many sports fans, I have a fascination with venues and how different they are from city to city, town to town, campus to campus. In Seattle, home of the country's coolest-setting for a college football stadium, I love the idea that fans take boats across Lake Washington to University of Washington's Husky Field, whose grandstands rise alongside the water like two cobras hissing at each other. In Tempe, Arizona, I love the red-rocked Tempe Butte rising beyond Sun Devils Stadium like something from a Roadrunner cartoon. In Fenway Park, I love, of course, the Green Monster in left field and how, instead of digital numbers, inning-by-inning scores are posted by a guy hanging wooden numbers.

When driving from Eugene to Corvallis on Peoria Road, I love the rusted backstop at Lake Creek Mennonite School, not much larger than a single-car garage door and the backdrop to softball games in which school girls wear dresses, head coverings and — this is so perfect — Nikes and Reeboks.

So, yes, because of the places games are played. But also because of the statistics. The numbers. On the players' backs. On a scoreboard. In a manager's mind. On a TV visual. On a rookie quarterback's wrist band. In a box score.

Numbers tell a story. In her book, *Wait Till Next Year* (see "A Fan's Favorite Books," Page 174) historian Doris Kearns Goodwin writes of listening to Red Barber's radio accounts of 1949 Brookyln Dodgers games and how, using the technique her father showed her, keeping scores of games. And writes of how, in a day when baseball was played only during the day, she would recount the games to her father at dinner.

"Well, did anything interesting happen today?" he would begin. And even before the daily question was completed I had eagerly launched in my narrative of every play, and almost every pitch, of that afternoon's contest ... Through my mastery as well as pleasure in our nightly ritual, I commanded my father's undivided attention, the sign of his love."

So, yes, we love sports because of the numbers, but also because of the history. The thought, before an Oregon State-Oregon football game, that these two teams have been hammering heads since 1894, when tailgating was a picnic-basket lunch on the back of a horse-and-buggy pulled snug to the sidelines. The thought that the Red Sox 2004 World Series championship was inextricably linked to 1918, the last time they accomplished as much. The thought that Slats Gill, for whom Oregon State's basketball arena was named, coached the Beavers from the start of the Great Depression (1929) until the arrival of The Beatles in America (1964).

Sportswriters would be lost without history. Coaches are far more concerned with this play, this game, this year. But writers love to compare and contrast — and history provides their context.

So, yes, because of the history. But also because of relationships, the people and how the games knit them together in some fashion.

It's baseball players emerging from an Iowa cornfield for a second shot. Players from the past drawn together, in *Field of Dreams*, by a game.

It's Brian Piccolo and Gale Sayers in *Brian's Song*, a white journeyman running back with cancer and a black man who's arrived to take his job. Two friends drawn together by a game.

It's my father and I playing knee football in our living room, me clutching a pair of socks that I pretend are a football and trying to score by reaching the couch, he rejecting me continuously as if his arms were a pair of pinball flippers. A father and son drawn together by a game.

It's the upper deck in some stadium, hundreds of people who arrive at their seats from lives far different from one another and yet, in a sense, check their demographics at the ticket gate. Different people drawn together by a game.

So, yes, we love sports because of the game. The game within a game. The strategy. The anticipation. The venues. The history. The relationships. And, of course, the unknown. It's the realization that when all these ingredients are fused together, we don't know what will happen, but it will be different every time and it will almost always be something good.

Like seeing your son standing on second base with a standup double against a pitcher a full head taller than him.

Ya gotta love that.

Civil War Lite

In November 2005, ESPN Radio, having read a column I'd written on the subject, asked if I would be interviewed that evening for their series on great football rivalries of America. I said sure, but added that I wasn't convinced the annual Beaver-Duck game, much as I enjoy it, qualifies as one of the great rivalries. It's gone on since 1894. It can be intense and, since 1997, when Oregon State's program finally found itself after decades of being lost in the football forest, is more intense now than it's been in decades. And a lot of Oregonians spout off about "the right to live in the state" stuff. But compared to some other rivalries, OSU-Oregon is really Rivalry Lite.

Beyond a few misguided souls who, say, swing dead ducks after a Beaver win (2000) or rip down and deposit goal posts in front of the OSU bench after a Duck win (1972), this isn't exactly Israel-Palestine.

Spend an evening at Eskimo Joe's in Stillwater, Oklahoma, listening to Oklahoma State fans explain how much they hate University of Oklahoma, and Oregon and Oregon State look like Sonny and Cher.

Here's why the rivalry is saner than many:

• Because the schools are only 40 miles apart, Ducks and Beavers have too much in common. We work, play, campaign, worship, eat and sleep with each other. The state is full of mixed marriages and parents with prodigal children who slink home in turncoat colors.

Like it or not, we have to get along with each other.

• Because both programs have gotten good, there's now life beyond the Civil War. How bad were they? In 1981, both entered the game with 1-9 records. In the old days, the Civil War was like two weakling brothers who routinely got beat up at school, then vented each year by thrashing each other in a pillow fight. Not that it was a very noble fight; in 1983, for example, they played to a pathetic 0-0 tie.

• Because we've gotten more technologically sophisticated, fans have foregone more spirited ways to manifest their dislike for one another. Most Civil War slams these days are spewed via e-mail; people let their fingers do the talking. It used to be fists. In 1910, fans clashed so violently that the 1911 game was canceled. "Fans were hitting each other over the head with pieces of the goal post," remembered the late John Warren, who played for Oregon in the '20s.

But even in 1937, when the Beavers paraded through Eugene after a win and were subsequently thrown in the millrace, there was a sense of levity to it. The *Oregon Daily Emerald* congratulated the Beavers for the "sportsmanlike" attack. The Beavers applauded the UO's millrace defense.

• Because the University of Washington exists, OSU can never be UO's No. 1 hate object. In one sense, that fuels the rivalry; it gets under the Beavers' fur that the UO doesn't think lowly enough of them. The Ducks would rather beat the Huskies than beat the Beavers. The Beavers would rather beat the Ducks than any team on Planet Earth. But the Ducks haven't been able to fully commit to Beaver distaste since 1948 when the Huskies' vote helped break a tie in the old Pacific Coast Conference, sending California to the Rose Bowl instead of the Ducks.

• Because Corvallis has gotten more liberal, the cultural chasm between the schools hardly exists. The Cow-U.-vs.-Hippie-U. image once contributed to the animosity. A Beaver win was a victory for Mom's Weekend, apple pie and the Greek system; a Duck win a triumph for Bob Marley, reefer madness and organic farming. But times change: In 2004, George Bush did slightly better in Lane County (40.6 percent) than he did in Benton (40.1). Who woulda thunk?

Because Beavers and Ducks are generally decent people, they put on their Civil War faces like Halloween masks, but are congenial to one another 51 weeks a year.

Goodness, Rich Brooks played football at Oregon State, coached at Oregon and was hired by former OSU Athletic Director Mitch Barnhart at Kentucky. UO's home-game announcer, Don Essig, was once an OSU cheerleader. And in the mid-'80s, retired OSU Athletic Director Dee Andros starred in two TV commercials to raise interest in Duck football. Yes, *Duck* football. In one, he danced. In the other, he lay in a hospital bed, with webbed feet, after suffering a "Quack Attack." Try that in Oklahoma or Texas or Birmingham, Alabama, and the coach would probably come home from the hospital to find his house torched.

So let's not apologize that our football wars are less barbaric than others. Let's celebrate it.

Civilly, of course.

Turkey Bowls

In the black-and-white photo, I'm standing on our back patio as a 10-year-old, a wet, baggy sweatshirt hanging on me like rain-forest moss. (See Page 55.) The sweatshirt's arms are so long — half-way between my waist and knees — that I look as if I'm Gumby without any hands. I'm wearing a pair of muddy football pants that balloon out at the bottom like the wax buildup at the base of a candle, giving me that George-walking-Mary-home-from-the-dance look in *It's a Wonderful Life*. The concrete patio is wet; this is, after all, winter in Oregon. The photo border says, "Nov. 64."

But, look more closely, and you realize it is the Mona Lisa of childhood photographs. For beyond all that bespeaks misery is an undeniable upward crease in my lips, a slight smile that conveys, if only to those who understand the sweet smell of winter mud, a historic truth:

I've just played in my first Turkey Bowl football game.

We all have our touchstones of the years, benchmarks that remind us that, for better or worse, we're growing older. Turkey Bowl football games are mine.

I am to Thanksgiving football games what the swallows are to Capistrano; I return to them faithfully, year after year, despite rain or hard rain (the only two Oregon options). I've played in them now for four decades. In fact, my Turkey Bowl life — like geologic time — can be separated into four eras: the Youth Era, the Macho Era, the Family Era and the Pathetic Era.

Beyond our muddy kids-vs.-kids games, the Youth Era meant two-generational street football — games that pitted us fleet-footed whip-persnappers against fortysomething has-beens. My father always played in wingtips. His passes fluttered like sick birds, but I'll say this: He got out there every year and gave it his best shot.

Next came the Macho Era, in which we home-from-college kids, now steeped in intellectualism, distanced ourselves from the Oppression of Family and once again played our own muddy games. Games accented by a touch of Oregon-Oregon State rivalry. Games in which, for all our freethinking new ways, winning became more important than life itself. Games in which the opposition was not only the man you were blocking — or, in my case, *pretending* to block — but your shoulder-length hair that kept getting in your way.

It was not, of course, enough to simply play the game: We had to publish our own eight-page newspaper, *The Turkey Bowl Tribune*, which was 90 percent trash-talking and 10 percent semi-trash talking. And, of course, take group photographs, one of which wound up on the cover of this book.

Soon we all went our separate ways to become doctors, accountants, Nike executives, attorneys, ministers, socialists, tree planters, journalists and cowboys singers who would ultimately be the opening act for Garth Brooks.

For me, the Family Era arrived; I had a wife and kids of my own, and on Thanksgiving the four of us continued the yearly tradition.

My fondest memory came after a Seattle TV news station offered to show scores of Turkey Bowl games. Being a benevolent father, I purposely took it easy on my sons so they would win. And there it was on the 6 o'clock KIRO sports news: Ryan & Jason 35, Mom & Dad 28. (Hey, I wasn't going to allow a wipeout.)

This Era also produced a post-game photograph (see Page 15) I'll never forget: Our younger son, Jason, then 4, is awash in the agony of defeat, tears streaking his face as if he's been stung by bees. Our then-7-year-old, Ryan, towers next to him, arms crossed, face smug: the Victorious Older Brother. My wife comforts her youngest with a mother's compassion.

Me? I'm safely behind the camera, being the guy who probably dropped the would-be game-winning pass that turned the tyke into emotional jelly.

Years later, I was playing opposite Ryan, then 12, in our church's annual Turkey Bowl when I nailed him with a beautiful block. He writhed in pain, the actual realness of which has been disputed each Thanksgiving since.

"He clipped me, he clipped me!" he screamed in his alleged anguish.

Players on both teams looked at him with wounded-puppy eyes, then turned to me as if I'd just robbed a Salvation Army Santa. (It was a clean block, I swear.)

The years passed. Times changed. I began showing up for games still nursing pulled muscles that I'd re-injured the previous year. My opponent would zig, I would zag, missing the tackle completely and slipping onto my anguished face. Once, I pulled into the parking lot before a game and there was the 19-year-old son of a friend of mine taking out his nose rings. I knew I was growing older.

Suddenly, I was the receiver the quarterback would throw a pass to only if the other 15 receivers (our church has big games) were covered. I was the fiftysomething has-been, the comedy act slipping around in tennis shoes while fearless teens in deep-cleated football shoes cut and slashed. When covering me, my sons purposely took it easy on me.

The Pathetic Era had arrived.

In recent years, I realized I was the oldest guy on the field — by nearly 10 years. My youth was, in Paul Simon-esque terms, slip-sliding away. Maybe it was time to hang up the mud-tinged tennies and spend Thanksgiving morning watching the Macy's parade, not falling face down in the mud.

Then came the e-mail recently that forced my decision. It was from John Mills, a good friend my age whom I'd played against in the Macho Era, a guy who could zip a wet, cold Turkey Bowl football like nobody I've ever seen. And had the mouth to back it up.

"I went out and threw the ball with my son the other day," he wrote, "and for the very first time since I was 13 years old, I did not feel like I could throw that thing with a spiral, velocity and accuracy. Very hard to accept this getting-older stuff."

Though simple, it touched something deep inside me. I realized the time had come. I was 50 years old. Time for a change. Time to do the only thing I could do, given the circumstances:

I bought a pair of football cleats.

I don't expect to keep up with the fleet-footed whippersnappers in this year's game, but it's Thanksgiving. No time to be sliding into remorse, lamenting that we're not what we once were.

Time, instead, to go out there like my father and give it my best shot. Time, instead, to be thankful for what we are — and still might be. Time for Turkey Bowls and the traditional post-game photo, last year's showing me surrounded by two grown sons, my face creased with mud.

And a smile that I haven't surrendered to the years.

The national anthem

Among the best 90 seconds of any sports event is the national anthem, provided it isn't sung by someone whose voice is to music what the '62 Mets were to baseball.

The anthem is one of those traditions of American sports that might be easily overlooked, something that's done so regularly that it gets taken for granted. But in the few games I've attended where it wasn't sung or played, the event seemed incomplete, like a marriage without a wedding.

For 90 seconds, whether we're in Section 314 or standing on the mound, whether we're a rich donor in sky suite or a wide-eyed kid who's only here because his foster mom spotted the 2-for-1 general-admission deal on Page E4 of that morning's paper, we're *one*.

For 90 seconds, we find ourselves invited to pause, to drink in the scene, to put it all in perspective. To remember that no matter how many days, weeks and months we've looked forward to this game, there's a larger world beyond.

For 90 seconds, we're afforded the opportunity to count our blessings: that we live in a place where people before us have fought for our freedom, a place where no matter the clutter of the world, we can escape to this park for an afternoon or evening of revelry and rivalry.

In a word, the national anthem reminds us of one thing: privilege.

To be here, in the United States. To be here, in this stadium. To be someplace where, in this sea of diversity around us, we share one thing in common. This quiet reminder that we are the fortunate ones.

As a columnist, I once had the privilege — for the most part— of sitting through 63 renditions of the national anthem in one afternoon. The University of Oregon was trying to decide which people and groups would be best to sing or play at its men's and women's basketball games that winter.

That's 95 minutes and 49 seconds of music if you're keeping score, which, of course, being a sports nut, I was.

It was hoop dreams meets "American Idol."

Somewhere along the way, it dawned on me that this was like another journalistic adventure I'd once had: judging a clam chowder contest in Seattle that required the tasting of nearly 100 restaurant samples.

The similarity? I had no idea the same entity could — for better or worse — be concocted in so many ways. The difference? I didn't leave Mac Court feeling like hurling.

In fact, I left feeling inspired, particularly by children so small that the on-stand microphone had to be bent toward them like a sagging sunflower.

I wasn't a judge, but I have a simple way of deciding whether *The Star-Spangled Banner* has been done well: If it has, you will instinctively want to start cheering when the song hits the "freeeeeeeeeee" near the end. If it hasn't, you won't.

Most contestants double-dribbled on the "rockets' red glare/bombs bursting in air" segment. A few high-pitched singers, in fact, threatened to shatter the glass backboards on those parts.

But, frankly, most contestants stood at that foul line, faced the five judges at midcourt and sank their shots. (The average song, by the way, lasted 1:31.35.)

Only a few people forgot words and, even then, the glitches were minor.

They were a diverse, if gutsy, bunch, mostly solo singers but also ensembles, gospel singers, small bands and a guitarist, violinist and horn player.

I'm sure they all had different reasons for wanting to do this. I'd

like to think that more than a few were there because they were drawn
not by the chance to be in the spotlight, but by the song itself. I'd like
to think they've even thought of the words:

> Oh, say can you see by the dawn's early light
> What so proudly we hailed at the twilight's last gleaming?
> Whose broad stripes and bright stars through the perilous fight,
> O'er the ramparts we watched were so gallantly streaming?
> And the rocket's red glare, the bombs bursting in air,
> Gave proof through the night that our flag was still there.
> Oh, say does that star-spangled banner yet wave
> O'er the land of the free and the home of the brave?

Nobody comes home from a game thinking how great *The Star
Spangled Banner* was. But there's something important about being
reminded that those ramparts were gallantly streaming. That, after
this battle, our flag was still there. And that we're still the land of the
free and the home of the brave.

At UO football games, near the end of the song, band members
sprint down the field, each with a red stripe that's been coiled up.
Others stream forward with blue to symbolize the stars. And I get
choked up. Every time.

Sometimes I think that's weird. It is, after all, just a song, right?
But, thinking it over, I decided I'd be more concerned if I didn't feel
some sort of emotion during that song.

Sports, after all, are about emotion. Not only during the games.
But in those few moments before, when we're reminded that, beyond
the field, we've faced some perilous fights. And won, though the
price was far higher than any athlete will ever pay.

The grip of golf

I return to golf courses to play golf for the reason, I suppose, that my late father returned to rivers to fish: to catch the one that got away. Or at least try. Somewhere out there, I'm convinced, is this 275-yard drive that will rise like an F-15 from the deck of an aircraft carrier, hang in the sky for what seems like minutes, then split the fairway with the precision of my mother cutting a peanut-butter sandwich cleanly in half when I was a boy. Somewhere out there is an approach shot that heads for the pin like a heat-seeking missile. Somewhere out there is a triple-breaking, downhill putt that I have never made but am utterly convinced I will.

Meanwhile, back at the reality ranch, I might duck-hook a drive into a blackberry thicket, nail my brother-in-law in the chest with an approach shot (as I did not long ago) and three-putt from 20 feet.

Lives there a sport that is more delicious and diabolical than golf?

I have spent my life immersed in sports. But golf holds a grip on me in a unique way.

Just as it is a complex game to play, so it is a complex game to understand. But not long ago, because of a slow group in front of our foursome, I found myself with 10 minutes to simply sit on a fairway mound and contemplate the meaning of golf. I was 210 yards away on a dogleg-left par-5 — water left of the green. Because I rarely have an opportunity to get home in two on such a hole, I was anxious to see if I could hit a 5-wood on the green and make birdie. And yet the moment was so quiet, so perfect, that I felt the unexpected peace of simply immersing myself in it.

We were playing a hillside gem called Diamond Woods in the heart of Oregon's Willamette Valley, a lush track carved through what once had been a Christmas tree farm. It was late October, a weekday afternoon. The sun would soon slip beyond the Coast Range, not only for the day, I sensed, but perhaps for months while Oregon went into its winter hibernation of clouds and drizzle.

This, then, is the allure of golf, the aesthetics you don't find in, say, a bowling alley: the sheer beauty of a golf course. Water and grass and trees and contour. Shade and slope and sun and light. And, of course, color, an array of color. An hour west of here, less than a mile from the crashing Pacific Ocean, you walk up the seventh fairway of Sand Pines Golf Course and, in one view, can see horizontal layers of color: the blue of the sky, the pale green of Douglas fir forests, the white of sand dunes, the vibrant green of the fairways — all sandwiched together like Neapolitan ice cream.

Here at Diamond Woods on this October afternoon, the course is framed in fall: oak and maple in their subtle oranges and yellows. The ponds are blue and so still that they beg you to pull out a rock and see if you can skip it clear across. A creek meanders through the woods; now shallow and spent by a dry summer, it will, by Christmas, be swift and cold.

It all begs you to connect not only with what my wife's grandmother loved to call "God's handiwork" but with one's self. We live in a noisy, fast-paced world. What simple joy to walk toward one's drive and simply feel free to think.

In a sense, you could say golf is an escape. But you could also say it's an escape to the profound: rest, relaxation, beauty and people we care about. When the guy on the adjacent fairway is getting ready to hit and his cell phone rings — well, perhaps that's the sound of a ball and chain, the world hounding him to return to the trivial.

As I survey the autumn scene, I see another reason that golf has a hold on me: My 20-year-old son, Ryan, home from college on a break, stands behind his drive on the other side of the fairway, 10 yards closer to the green than me.

I am one of those people who has enjoyed playing golf by myself. As a boy, I would, on uncrowded days, play two balls and pit Arnie (Palmer) vs. Jack (Nicklaus). But I also loved the way golf lends itself to relationships. To small talk. To occasional big talk. And, of course, to the proverbial banter of guys whose talk is usually more impressive than their swings.

When Ryan was 15, we awoke one August morning just before dawn in my grandfather's beach cabin. We drove seven miles north, walked onto the beach, sunk a soup can in the sand, then put a branch with a seaweed "flag" on it. We then drove back to the cabin, took out our drivers and, just as the sun hinted its arrival, teed off on our creation: a 7-mile-long golf hole.

It was a par-72, we decided, and, ironically, we both shot four-under-par 68s. But the real value of the endeavor had nothing to do with balls and clubs and scores, and everything to do with fathers and sons. With a relationship.

It is hard to relate with someone when you're trying to cut them off on the baseline or tackle them or throw them out at first base. But golf offers the opportunity for people to connect.

Golf, in that sense, is a gentleman's sport. A player's competitive fires can be burning deep inside and yet the interaction between two golfers can be completely civil. To be sure, exceptions exist, but more than other sports, golf seems to breed a certain spirit of cooperation between players. We help each other look for a lost ball. We give each other yardages. We tend the pin for one another.

What's more, golf breeds a sense of honor in that players police themselves. I'm not naive enough to believe all golfers live up to that code, but most do. Once, in a round of golf in which we were both playing poorly enough that cutting a few strokes here and there wouldn't have been noticed by the other guy, my brother-in-law hacked around in the trees, finally found the green, rolled in a putt and announced he'd had a "14." I've seen professional golfers call two-stroke penalties on themselves simply because their ball moved as they addressed it with their club. Honor is important and golf helps breed it.

As I awaited my shot on this October afternoon, I realized that daylight was going fast; with 10 holes to play, we would probably play the final few holes in near darkness and might even wish we had one of those airport ground-crew guys with their flashlights to guide us home. This, too, is the appeal of golf; it's ever changing. The course looks different now than it will look an hour from now.

In April, I would not be going for the green in two. In April, my drive would have plugged 30 yards back and I would be laying up with a 5-iron and playing safe for par. Golf is governed by ever-changing elements.

Weather, of course, is one of them. Recently, I played an Oregon beach-side course, Bandon Dunes, that golf magazines are saying is the rival of Pebble Beach. Having played both, I agree. But a 30 mph wind meant sometimes hitting a 4-iron in a situation where I'd normally hit a 9-iron. It was British Open golf with a Southern twist: My scores were gone with the wind.

Golf courses are never the same twice. A 15-foot putt on a dewy morning will be slower and break less than that same putt in the afternoon. On this day, the tees were up, the pin left-center; tomorrow, on this same hole, the tees may be back and the pin right-front.

But I digress. The foursome ahead of us has putted out. It is time, finally, for The Shot. My two friends and son watch as I take my stance and prepare to swing. The flag, back-left on a kidney-shaped green, teases me. Draw the ball even slightly and my Titleist will find a watery grave. Miss the green right and I'll be hitting over a series of camel-back mounds.

This is what golf does so well: tests you, dares you, challenges you. On a shot like this, it doesn't matter whether I'm Tiger Woods or the 18-handicapper that I am. I have a sense of opportunity, of possibility, of potential. The beauty of the moment is so perfect — the scenery, the weather, the playing partners and, of course, the opportunity. I feel as if anything but a perfect shot will spoil it all, like falling when water-skiing on glass-smooth water.

The time has come. I swing hard and like the feel of the contact. I have struck the ball well. Alas, my water worries apparently have sent the subliminal message to my body to keep the ball right. It flies right of the green, bounces hard on a mound and kicks into an adjacent fairway — pin high, but 40 yards away.

There is nothing better than seeing a well-struck shot go where you intended it. But as I walk to the ball, I don't sense dejection. For the golf experience is so much more than a single shot, or even the sum total of all those shots that culminate with two or three numbers:

69, 83, 98, 108 ... .

The golf experience is the sound of a Canada goose in the distance as you stand over a putt and the way a son's arm punches the sky when he sinks a birdie, and the camaraderie between your foursome as you wait to hit. The score isn't the fullest expression of the experience; it lies much deeper, in what you'll remember about the day when you're hibernating in that Oregon winter.

Besides, before I loft a wedge over the mounds and make a pretty decent two-putt for par, I have already decided something during this late-season round: I'll be back. As my father would say, you have to go after the one that got away.

Thus, do we return to the river. Thus, do we return to the course.

— From *Where the Grass is Always Geener.*
Copyright ©: Paintings by Donny Finley, text compiled by Terry Glaspey.
Published by Harvest House Publishers, Eugene, Oregon
Used by permission.

Unquenchable thirst

The most fascinating interview I've ever had with an athlete was with Alberto Salazar, at one time the greatest marathoner on Earth. We sat in the living room of his home, Casa de Salazar, perched high on a hill overlooking much of the city of Eugene, the self-proclaimed running capital of the world.

What made it so fascinating was that Salazar, nearly a decade after winning three straight New York Marathons and breaking the Boston Marathon record, dared to bare his soul about the most profound part of sports: winning.

In two afternoons of interviews — he was also the most accommodating big-name athlete I've interviewed — Salazar revealed something that astounded me: at the peak of his career, when he could run 26 miles, 385 yards faster than any human being on the planet, Alberto Salazar was a man in anguish.

Self-driven to succeed, he could not be content without being the best, but neither could he be content after becoming the best. He was a man who seemingly created his own destiny, then watched it crumble. A man whose lack of peace gnawed at him like a runner's cramp that wouldn't go away.

Winning, it seems, was never enough. "It was a cycle," he said, looking back. "The more I achieved, the more I wanted. There was always one more step. Even if I won an NCAA championship, I'd say, 'Now I'll get a gold medal, now I'll set a world record, or now I'll beat the world record.'"

Whereas most runners rest in the days following a big race, Salazar would hit the road the next morning for 20 hard miles. He once put in a 100-mile-a-week summer — with a stress fracture. If Salazar ran 10,000 meters in 27 minutes and 45 seconds, it didn't matter that he'd won and set a meet record; if he were shooting for 27:30, he would smile his way around a few victory laps, then enter the locker room seething. "I would hate that. I would feel I failed."

Winning is the great paradox of sports. Whether reflected in the Super Bowl or a coach-pitch youth game, American culture views being No. 1 as a sacred achievement, the ultimate goal, the main reason we compete. But with all due respect to the late Vince Lombardi, winning isn't everything.

Winning is a worthy goal; a summer doesn't pass that I don't drive past the Shasta Middle School ball fields and picture my youngest son's last-inning poke to center field, wishing that the outfielder hadn't made a diving catch to thwart our comeback attempt and end the championship game, 4-2.

Winning is much more fun than losing. I should know; I played on a City League basketball team that went 0-for-three-years, though we did take a team into overtime before losing our 30th and last game.

But in itself, winning isn't enough; the cost-to-benefit ratio is too high. It can't compensate for children so stressed by sports that they grind their teeth at night. Parents so intent on turning their children into superstars that they sacrifice the family in the process. And athletes so obsessed with being the best that it carries over into their nonathletic life.

In their book, *Winning and Other American Myths*, psychologist Thomas Tutko and writer William Bruns put it in terms to which Alberto Salazar could relate:

> Winning is like drinking salt water; it will never quench your thirst. It is an insatiable greed. There are never enough victories, never enough championships or records ... .

There's a difference between giving an all-out effort to win and being obsessed with winning.

Winning has become an obsession when a Babe Ruth baseball coach — as happened in my fair city recently — is caught using a college-aged assistant coach as a designated hitter.

Winning has become an obsession when a Little League coach in Southern Oregon gives his players $5 for every base hit in an All-Star game.

Winning has become an obsession when, midway through a season, a team — like one I saw recently — loses its desire to even play because they've been made to feel like failures by their win-or-else coach.

We are becoming an increasingly results-oriented, rather than process-oriented, culture. Outcome has become everything; the experience has become nothing.

Once, while coaching youth baseball, our team got trounced in a game that, according to league rules, had to be called after four innings because the margin was 10 runs. The umpires left. Parents started to leave.

I was stunned: In essence, we were saying that a baseball game has no value unless it is close; that it's so humiliating to be behind by 10 runs that it's better to not continue the very reason these kids turned out in the first place: to play. To have fun. To compete.

As people headed for their cars, I thought about how my team had worked hard all week in practice and had been rewarded by this: A rule that said you can't play because you're not good enough. I grabbed two parents who agreed to be umpires, went to the other coach, and suggested we keep playing — with the understanding, of course, that officially the game was over and his team had won 12-2.

He shrugged and said OK. Most parents returned to their seats. A parent-turned-umpire called "play ball" and one of the opposing team's batters stepped into the box.

Then the batter said something that has haunted me ever since. "Coach," he yelled to the burly man in the third-base box. "Are we just playing for fun now?"

I've never heard a sadder commentary on children and sports in my life. As adults, we should be ashamed when we allow sports to become so win-oriented that young people think the "fun light" only goes on once their game or practice is over. The "fun light" should go on the minute their game or practice begins, because fun — pure, unadulterated play — is the truest essence of sports. Otherwise, let's just call it war or business or politics or something worse.

On the flip side, one of the most beautiful moments I've ever seen in sports at the tail-end of a recent high school girls' basketball game. The two teams had traded one-point leads for nearly the entire fourth quarter and finally two guards who had been dogging each other all night wound up going one-on-one. Three … two … one … The offensive player fired a do-or-die shot to win the game. It missed.

Then, the moment: The two girls, both physically and emotionally spent, instinctively hugged each other — as if sports for them went far beyond which red bulbs were lit up on a scoreboard, went to something deeper, something in the soul: in this case, respect for one another and, perhaps, pride in a battle well fought.

I recently saw a young man slide into third and accidentally spike the third baseman in the knee. Moments later, he helped carry his opponent to the dugout. That young man saw beyond the scoreboard.

A colleague and I once ran a 10K road run. We agreed before the race that we would run the first five miles together, then go our separate ways if one was feeling stronger than the other. At the five-mile mark, I pulled away. But near the finish, he passed me, gave me a word of encouragement and wound up finishing ahead of me. A few days later, he walked into my office with a jar of homemade strawberry jam. "You pulled me along for most of the race," he said. "Thanks." He saw beyond the stopwatch.

My son, Ryan, was coaching a youth sports playoff game that went into overtime. In the extra period, I was surprised to see him put in the shortest, least-skilled player for a few minutes. After the game, which his team had won, I questioned him about the move.

"It's just a YMCA basketball game, Dad," he said. "The kid hadn't gotten to play, so I put him in." My son saw beyond wins and losses.

Competition is the hub on which the athletic wheel turns. But we are to compete for the right reasons. What's important here isn't our perfection, but our purpose.

I once wrote a letter to encourage a friend, a coach whose enthusiasm for the game seemed gone, his frustration at losing manifesting itself in uncharacteristic fits of courtside rage. "Sometimes I get so caught up in the race," he wrote back, "that I forget why I entered."

Sometimes, it takes a child to remind us that it's the journey, not the outcome or stopwatch, that matters most. At an all-comers track meet in Eugene, a 7-year-old finished fourth in the 220-yard dash.

"How fast did you run?" asked an adult.

"As fast as I could," he replied, eyes wide.

If you can fill the unforgiving minute
With sixty seconds' worth of distance run,
Yours is the Earth and everything that's
in it ...

— Rudyard Kipling

2
The
Athlete

The author after his first Turkey Bowl, November 1964, in Corvallis. Age 10. (Warren Welch)

The chosen one

O n a December morning in 1969, dozens of sophomore boys at Corvallis High walked to the corner of the school gym and looked at a list posted on the wall. Those whose names were on the list were the Chosen Ones, 14 guys who would proudly don the powder blue and white Spartans uniforms to represent the school as its sophomore boys' basketball team.

Mine wasn't on it.

I scanned up and back like the frantic mother in *The Deep End of the Ocean* looking for her kidnapped child in the hotel lobby — knowing, deep inside, my name wasn't there but figuring if I looked hard enough, I could will it to appear. But my name wasn't on that list.

When reality set in, there was only one thing to do: Dabble in denial. There must be some mistake. Mr. Kinney, the varsity coach who had final say on all the teams, must have typed the alphabetical list the previous night and right after he'd typed Matt Wahl's name, he'd gotten distracted by something on *Rowan & Martin's Laugh-In*. When he resumed his list-making, he hopped from Wahl to Yastrop, accidentally forgetting Welch. An innocent mistake; anyone could have made it.

Naw. There was no mistake.

When acceptance set in, there was only one thing to do: complain. Rail at the unfairness of life. Question the selections. One guy who made the team hadn't even been a starter on his junior high team as I had. Another couldn't fight his way out of a phone booth, much less get through a double screen.

But in the game of life, I'd been benched. Blame it on my 5-foot-6 height. With the exception of Mark Lasswell, a small guy who played with the intensity of a Chipmunk song, everyone on this team was roughly half a foot taller than me. In the last year, it was as if every kid my age had gotten on this bus whose marquee said "Puberty" and I was left back at the Greyhound station while some kind-hearted clerk said, "Don't worry, son. There'll be another bus by in a couple years. You can take it."

This wasn't fair. This was worse than the day during seventh-grade lunch when the going-steady ring I'd given Lowrey Beam came sliding down the cafeteria table, stopping near my fish sticks and Jell-O as if to mockingly say: *It's over, pal. You're history.*

As I walked down the hallway to my first-period class, that's how I felt. Like I was history. Like my athletic career was over at age 15. Like everyone in the hallway was looking at me and whispering: "Did you hear? He got cut."

But later that morning, something happened that would ultimately change everything. I was sitting in Mrs. Shaw's English class — I wonder if Shakespeare ever got cut from his sophomore basketball team? — when a student office-worker politely interrupted the class to hand me a written message.

Normally, such messages spelled doom. Emergencies. Someone in your family had been in an accident or the principal had caught wind that it was you who, during the Christmas concert, had paid Mark Baker the $20 to cluck like a chicken while doing a loop around the choir during "We Three Kings."

But I liked the timing on this one: Cuts posted this morning; message arrives an hour later. What I liked even better was the message itself: See Coach Kinney ASAP.

My sunken spirits rebounded. My imagination headed down court on a torrid fast break:

" ... as I said, I'm sorry, Bob, I must have gotten distracted by something on *Laugh-In* ..."

Or maybe: " ... and after thinking it over, I've decided to take 15 boys, not 14 ..."

Or perhaps: " ... you've probably heard the tragic news about Mike Nelson having mononucleosis, meaning we need to replace him immediately ... ."

Suddenly, there I was, not surmising what Coach Kinney might say but actually sitting in the man's office, the office of the legendary varsity coach who had led Corvallis High to the state tournament with the regularity of spring itself.

"Bob," he said, "nobody hustled out there during tryouts more than you did."

Hallelluah! The man had come to his senses.

"You gave 110 percent at every practice."

So true, coach, but enough of this prelude; just tell me I'm going to be donning the Spartan powder blue and white. Just say it like this coach: "Bob, how would you like to be on the sophomore basketball team?"

Coach Kinney ran a hand back through his crew cut and looked me dead in the eye.

"Bob," he said, "how would you like to be our junior varsity manager?"

Huh? It was as if someone suddenly pulled the plug on the jukebox of life. The music died. My world stopped spinning. My head tilted slightly forward in disbelief, my eyes unbelieving.

JV manager?

A pause ensued, the kind of perplexing pause that happens when life zigs when you expected it to zag.

What could I say? What I wanted to say was: Hold everything. Timeout, ref. What's going on here? Wrong call.

JV manager? This was like opening the largest, coolest-wrapped present under the Christmas tree and finding a rust-colored cardigan sweater knit by your grandmother, complete with outlines of the original 13 states on back.

JV manager? This was like wanting to be a movie director and instead selling popcorn and those industrial-sized boxes of Dots at the local twelve-plex.

"If you were a foot taller, you'd be out on that court yourself," the coach said, "But, Bob, every successful basketball team has a go-to guy, a manager who, well, is almost like a member of the team itself."

Right. Except while the players are running and gunning and having fun, this manager guy is keeping the shots-attempted chart and getting a sweat-top flung in his face.

"You'd be at every practice, travel with the team, eat meals with us, the works."

Gee, I've always wondered what it's like picking up towels in some exotic locker room like, say, the one at Sweet Home, built shortly after Lewis & Clark arrived in this neck of the woods.

"So, what do you think, Bob? I think you'd make a great manager."

"Well, I, uh, was hoping" — the coach's eyes grew a tad larger and he slowly nodded his head in encouragement. "Uh, sure," I said. "I'll do it."

He stuck out his hand. "Great," he said. "Welcome to the team."

I became the JV manager. I washed 12 basketballs before every practice. I rebounded for free-throw drills. I handed out uniforms. I made sure the water bottles were full. I kept statistics. I picked up towels.

Our coach was Chris Christianson, a short man with a sardonic wit, elfin-like features and a bow tie. He taught biology and seemed to think I was OK. We all called him Mr. Chris.

The players all called me "Bob." As in, "Bob, can I get a Band-Aid?" or, more formally, "Hey, Bob, what was my field goal percentage tonight?" But they seemed to like and respect me, partly because I knew a little bit about the game of basketball and partly because I was a sportswriter on the *High-O-Scope*, the student paper, and they knew I could blemish their young careers with a few clicks of my Smith-Corona.

Occasionally, I'd get in a pick-up game with some of the guys. I didn't want to be passing out towels for next year's JV team; I wanted to be the passee. I wanted to be proudly wearing the powder blue and white. So I needed to keep practicing.

The season began. All three teams — varsity, JV and sophomores — started winning basketball games and having fun in the process. Early in the season, the varsity blew out an opponent 117-61 and people started talking about how this was it — this was the year we might take state, something we'd never done before.

After the JVs would play, I got to watch every varsity game. Huge crowds packed each game — even on the road as opponents tried to stall the Spartan steamroller.

But nobody could. The varsity won 10 in a row, then stretched the streak to 15, 20, 21. Finally, it was the last regular game of the season for all three teams: The varsity was 21-0, the JVs 18-2 and the Sophomores 18-3.

Because we were playing our arch-rival Albany and a huge crowd was expected, the varsity and JV games were shifted to Oregon State University's Gill Coliseum. Everything was set for the crowning touch to our sensational season: Playing the dasterdly Albany Bull-dogs in the final game on the same floor where some of the country's greatest collegiate players, such as UCLA's Kareem Abdul-Jabbar (then Lew Alcindor), had played.

One slight problem: At halftime, our JV team was down by 10 points to a team we had beaten easily earlier in the season. Except for the faint sound of the pep band, the locker room was dead quiet as the 14 players sat on the benches. Mr. Chris stared at the floor. I stood off to the side, towel in hand.

Mr. Chris had a temper and I had a feeling the volcano was about to blow. Sure enough, he launched into a red-faced tirade, the kind of speech he must have heard a hundred times back in boot camp. He paused to mentally reload.

"You know what bothers me most?" There was a pause, each kid, like me, undoubtedly drawking a blank. "You guys don't even care! You act like you don't even wanna be out there! Like you're too worried about who you're taking to the dance tomorrow night! Like you don't even care about the game of basketball! Well let me tell you, it's a privilege to play basketball! A *privilege!*"

Another pause. He had softened 'em up with an aerial attack. Now he was going to bring in the ground troops. He was going to say something inspirational. He was going to say something that reached to the core of their souls. He was going to say —

"You see that kid over there?" the coach said, not in my mind but to everyone in that lockerroom.

Huh? He pointed to me. Fourteen heads turned my way.

"Gentlemen," he said slowly, "I've got a manager over there who would give his left *testicle* to be out there on that floor in Spartan blue, playing the game that you don't seem to give a rip about. Think about it."

Believe me, I was.

I wanted to say, "Who, me?" I wanted to say, "Uh, coach, it's true that I love the game, but ...." I wanted to say, "I know you mean well, Mr. Chris, but next time you might wanna clear some of your motivational examples with me ... ."

But Coach Kinney, the man who had hired me for this hallowed position, had been right. I wasn't just the manager. I was, well, like a member of the team. So I just pursed my lips a bit and nodded my head slowly, as if it to say: "Yep, fellas, Coach is right. So whataya gonna do about it?"

What they did about it was go out and absolutely thrash Albany in front of the largest crowd that had ever seen a JV basketball game in the history of Corvallis High. It was among the most amazing displays of Jekyll-and-Hyde athleticism I would see in decades of watching sports, a comeback for the ages.

The varsity went on to win all its games to become the first team in the state of Oregon to go undefeated en route to the Class AAA championship: twenty-six wins, no losses. After the championship game, fans drove the two hours from Portland to Corvallis where the parents of one of our star players opened their ice cream shop up at midnight to celebrate.

There had never been a varsity basketball season like that one in the history of our school, nor has there been one since. And I saw every one of those victories. Rode on the same bus with these guys. And, of course, became the George Gipp of JV halftime talks, the star of a story that still gets told at an occasional high school reunion, along with the football story about linebacker Ken Maddox accidentally intercepting a pass when a hard-thrown ball wedged between his facemask and helmet.

But there's more:

In a world big on getting, I learned how to give a little more that winter. In a world big on power, I learned how to serve a little more. In a world big on pride, I learned how to humble myself a little more. At the time, I can't say I noticed such profundity in my midst, but life's lessons sometimes bear fruit well after the season in which they are planted.

I never did wear the powder blue and white of a Spartan basketball uniform. Nor did I hand out another towel. I didn't even make the yearbook photo as JV manager, having been sick the day the photographer came. But I'll always remember the winter of 1969-70 as a time when I learned that, even when your name isn't on the list, life goes on.

The gift

The time you won your town the race
We chaired you through the market place;
Man and boy stood cheering by,
And home we brought you shoulder-high.

Today the road all runners come,
Shoulder-high we bring you home,
And set you at your threshold down
Townsman of a stiller town.

Smart lad, to slip betimes away
From field where glory does not stay
And early though the laurel grows
It withers quicker than the rose ....

— From A.E. Houseman's poem,
To an Athlete Dying Young

I heard the news on one of those sunny spring mornings that, at least in Oregon, you wish you could Select All, Copy and Paste to replace some drizzly January day six months hence.

I was heading into the University of Oregon's Allen Hall, home of the School of Journalism, when a friend greeted me not with his usual hello but with a chilling question.

"Did you hear about Pre?"

"Hear what?"

"He's dead."

Steve Prefontaine, at only 24 the greatest distance runner in America, had been killed in a car accident shortly after midnight. He had missed a turn on Hendricks Hill, less than two miles from campus, and rammed his sports car into a rocky outcropping. It had flipped and pinned him underneath.

Impossible. As a sportswriter on the campus paper, I had just seen him win the 5,000 meters in a track meet the previous night. I had watched as he jogged his traditional victory lap to celebrate his 25th straight win, the crowd of 7,000 fans at UO's Hayward Field applauding their hero with "Go-Pre!" gusto.

Impossible. A week later, I was sitting in those same Hayward Field stands at a memorial for him. No victory lap this time, only remembrances of an athlete dying young. The stadium clock ran as we sat in silence; it would stop at 12 minutes and 36 seconds, a world record for three miles with which Pre would have been well satisfied.

As the seconds clicked away to commemorate this life, so did my memories of Pre ....

I first saw Steve Prefontaine on a cool spring evening in 1969 while attending the Corvallis Invitational track meet in my hometown. I was a ninth-grader in my second year as a miler. I was a hack, a kid who had realized he was too light for football, too short for basketball, too slow for the sprints and yet too passionate about sports to not find some way to compete.

Pre, three years my senior, was all that I was not: fast, gutsy, charismatic — a kid from Coos Bay, a small, blue-collar community on the Oregon Coast, who was starting to run times that had race officials staring at their stopwatches in disbelief.

I remember the buzz in the stands as No. 13, the slight kid in black shorts and a white Marshfield High top, pulled away from the field that evening in the two-mile:

"... The kid has no fear ... ."

"... Sixty-eight-second first lap ... ."

"... Record pace ... ."

The race was the meet's second-to-last event and the April darkness only added to the drama as Pre, far ahead of his competitors, raced the clock.

"It's within reach," somebody with a stopwatch said. "The American record!"

As Pre pushed the pace lap after lap, we realized we were in the midst of greatness — on a small high school track, a touch of sports history was unfolding before our eyes.

Down home stretch he flew, breaking the tape and collapsing into the arms of his coach, Walt McClure. Prefontaine had broken the national high school two-mile record by more than seven seconds, clocking 8:41.5. I cut out the article from the next day's *Corvallis Gazette-Times* and filed it in a manila folder marked "To Remember." Thirty-seven years later, I still have it.

Pre would go on to complete his high school career without having lost a single race in Oregon his junior and senior years. As a college freshman, he made the cover of *Sports Illustrated* — "America's Distance Prodigy, Freshman Steve Prefontaine." In the photo, which I proudly displayed in my bedroom as part of my *Sports Illustrated* "wallpaper," he was shown running alone on a hill outside Eugene, overlooking the McKenzie River. He was now wearing the green and yellow of the University of Oregon, the home-state college that he had chosen because its legendary coach, Bill Bowerman, had written Pre a note that spoke the same kind of bravado that fueled Pre's passion to succeed: If Prefontaine came to Oregon, Bowerman had hand-scrawled, he would become the greatest distance runner ever.

Therein lay the Prefontaine mystique. It wasn't just that he was a young man blessed with speed and stamina, nor even that he was an unlikely hero, a man cheered by thousands but who lived in a rusted trailer and lived on food stamps. It was that he took "The Gift," as he called it, and dared to carry it as far as he possibly could. "To give anything less than your best," he would tell young athletes at clinics and camps, "is to sacrifice The Gift."

He didn't care how unrealistic it was for a slight kid from a tiny Oregon lumber town to even think about being the best runner in the world; instead, he fixed his eyes on a dream, toed the line, and, once the gun went off, never looked back.

What he looked at was the clock. If there's an image of Prefontaine frozen in the minds of those who saw him run, it's the image of him rounding the final turn and taking a passionate glance at the stadium clock on the far side of the track.

Prefontaine loved to win and hated to lose, but he seemed to run for another purpose, as if he needed to win in a place deep within himself, a place that transcended the race results, a place few of us dare to pursue for fear we might not reach it.

In addition to his desperate drive to succeed, what added to the Prefontaine mystique were the elements of time and place. As the '60s became the '70s, America was fighting two wars — one in Vietnam with bullets and bazookas, the other back home with angry words and violent anti-war protests. Amid the Kent States and Watergates of the era, Prefontaine emerged as a kid whose all-out style could take you away from four dead in Ohio and White House lies. We needed a hero; Prefontaine eagerly obliged.

What's more, he emerged in Eugene, the hallowed home of distance running, where an unprecedented 26 runners have run four-minute miles; where Olympic Trials, NCAA and national meets have been held with regularity; where coaches such as Bowerman and Bill Dellinger groomed distance runners with a sort of homespun approach that mirrored the earthiness of Oregon itself; and where Nike was born, Bowerman using his wife's waffle iron to create the first rubber soles.

Amid it all, Prefontaine reigned as this mop-haired role model for runners everywhere. At Corvallis High, on the same track where Prefontaine had burst onto the national scene in 1969 with his record two-mile, I can still remember our cross-country coach bellowing at us before a workout: "Hey, let's get ready, guys. Stretch out. You don't see Pre standing around like this."

No, what you saw Pre doing was taking off at the sound of a gun and never looking back; he simply ran away from the competition. You saw him waving to his beloved fans in Eugene, where he won 35 of the 38 races he ran. And you saw him occasionally popping off to reporters — and, at times, to spectators.

Pre was good, and he knew it. In 1973, during a dual meet between Oregon and Oregon State in Corvallis, I was sitting in the stands with a friend who went to OSU and had little love for anything related to the sinister UO. For some reason, Pre ran the three-mile that day instead of dropping down to run the mile against Oregon State's Hailu Ebba, an Ethiopian with incredible speed and stamina.

After Ebba clocked a track-record 3:58.1, my friend spouted to anyone within earshot: "It's a good thing Pre didn't race Ebba, 'cause he woulda got smoked."

"Bull," retorted someone nearby, only with a tad more spice. We looked down the row and there he was, Prefontaine himself, giving my friend a laser look.

At times, intensity works against people when they let it go too far; at times, Pre's ego got the best of him. After failing to set a record in a meet in California, his post-meet moaning all but blamed the citizens of Fresno for allowing there to be too much wind.

When I arrived on the Oregon campus as a freshman in 1972, Pre was among the first interviews I did for the college newspaper. It was an early-morning phone interview that won't go down as one of my more fascinating one-on-one sessions, but Prefontaine was Prefontaine: brash, impatient and to the point.

Just like he ran. In the 1972 Olympic 5,000-meter race in Munich, Prefontaine faced the toughest field he would ever run against. At age 21, the youngest in a 13-man race, he was going toe to toe with such international greats as Lasse Viren of Finland, who had set a world record in the 10,000 meters earlier in the games.

Pre wanted an all-out race in which the winner would simply be "who's toughest." He wanted a guts race, a Coos Bay race. What he got instead was international politics, a sluggish game of cat and mouse by runners with far more political savvy than he had. Finally, with four laps to go, Pre forced the pace with 62.5-second and 61.2-second laps, far faster than the 67-pace the field was on; Prefontaine was either going to win the gold medal or die trying.

Spent after twice being rebuffed while trying to pass on the final lap, Prefontaine reached for something more on the home stretch, but it wasn't there. He struggled home in fourth place. Viren won in a time four seconds slower than Prefontaine's Olympic Trials time.

Pre was crushed. But slowly he forgot about the past and began focusing on the future. He went unbeaten as a college senior, won an unprecedented fourth straight NCAA three-mile championship and, in the next two years, tested himself against the best international competition there was.

Now, when he came around the final corner of a race, his eyes were not only on the stadium clock, but on the 1976 Olympics in Montreal and a rematch with Viren and the others.

Alas, he died trying.

Hours before his death, he had been at a party that drew some of the national and international stars who had raced that evening. The autopsy results, after his 1973 MGB hit the rocky outcropping, would show that Pre's blood-alcohol level was above the Oregon legal driving limit.

Would he have become, as Bowerman once promised, the greatest distance runner ever? Perhaps. Most runners don't reach their primes until 25; Bowerman purposely held Prefontaine back, he said, so he would peak in his late 20s.

The world will never know. Viren went on to win the 5,000 and 10,000 meters in Montreal and to place fourth in the marathon — an incredible triple that suggests Pre may never have been the world's best. But for a guy like me whose greatest glory was a 4:59.8 all-comers mile on the same track Pre averaged 4:21 for *two* miles — the runner remains an inspiration.

I sometimes run across "Pre's Trail" alongside the Willamette River and through forests of firs to the top of Hendricks Hill. My route often takes us by the rocky outcropping where Pre took his last breath. "Pre's Rock" it's called.

Even now, people still leave their race numbers on the rock, sometimes a pair of running shoes, sometimes a poem. Which makes me wonder: What did Pre leave for us?

I'm not sure what he left for others. But for me, what he left was something I've had in my mind's "To Remember" file for a quarter of a century: the encouragement to take "The Gift" and to make of it all that we can — to fix our eyes on that dream and, once the gun goes off, to never look back.

Trading places

Every now and then I think back to something in my past and say to myself: Did I really do that? It's not as if my past could create a 10-part miniseries on boyhood evil, but just the same, directors would be hard-pressed to fit it all in a two-hour docudrama.

One incident, in particular, has dogged me over the years, an incident in which my motives seemed innocent enough at the time and yet triggered something tragic.

It was the fall of 1968 and I was a reserve halfback for the Cheldelin Junior High football team. As time slipped by, I would remember three things about that season.

First, that we got to practice on grass instead of sawdust. The school was in only its second year and the previous season, because our grass hadn't yet been planted, we'd practiced in sawdust for three months. And itched for three months. And heard our mothers complain about sawdust in their washing machines for three months.

Second, that I scored an extra point — my only score ever in organized tackle football — in our stunning 19-6 upset of Western View. I was a second-team running back and my scrapbook statistics — kept in a manila folder labeled "Memories" — show I carried the ball three times for five yards, an impressive 1.67-yards-per-carry average. I played so little that, along with fellow scrub Cortney Burris, I would rub mud on my thigh pads so when the game was over, our fans — particularly the young female fans — might think I'd actually seen action. But against Western View, in a game in which our star linebacker John Nordyke had swallowed up running backs like an alligator pursuing wounded ducks, I was thrown in at the end of the game, given a hand-off, and somehow scored an extra point, a feat which seems all the more remarkable considering I think I ran those three yards with my eyes closed.

And finally, I remember that I did something I've always regretted. It came during a routine drill called the meat grinder. It was simple: There were two lines, offense and defense, runners and tacklers. A runner was tossed the ball and a kid from the other line came up and tackled him. One on one. Pride vs. pride — all of it done in front of a couple of coaches and about two dozen teammates, hootin' and hollerin'.

As I waited my turn in the running back line, I did what any self-respecting 110-pound halfback concerned about his immediate future would do: I counted ahead to see what defensive player I would draw.

John Nordyke. (Cue *Dragnet* theme.)

Perhaps I'd miscounted. *Please, Lord, may I have miscounted.* Nope. A recount showed I was the seventh offensive player and Nordyke was the seventh defensive player.

John Nordyke was Mr. Mellow off the field and a monster on it. What frightened me wasn't so much that he outweighed me by a good 50 pounds and was 5-foot-10 to my 4-foot-11. What frightened me was thinking about times he'd hit ball carriers so hard that their helmets popped off like champagne corks.

Sizing up the situation, I did what any self-respecting conniver would do: I turned to the running back behind me, Ricky Root, and casually asked if he would like to trade places. In retrospect, it was like a passenger on the *Titanic* politely asking to borrow a life jacket from a passenger who hadn't heard the news yet.

Like me, Ricky Root was a second- or third-stringer. Unlike me, though, he wasn't the kind of wimp who would actually count ahead to see what defender he might be facing in the meat grinder drill. Nor was he the kind of guy who would stop to wonder why I might be asking that sort of question. I don't remember much about him, other than that he had gone to Mountain View grade school, which is one of the district's poorer, rural schools. For some reason, I sensed he'd had a pretty tough upbringing.

"Trade places?" he asked.

"Yeah," I said.

"Sure," he said. "Why not?"

For a few moments, I felt a little like I imagine Houdini felt when he had once again cheated death. There I had been, handcuffed inside the chain-secured coffin, 60 feet beneath the East River in freezing temperatures and, suddenly, I was on the surface, alive!

"Root vs. Nordyke," yelled Coach Osborne. His whistle blew. Nordyke bolted forward like a rodeo bull uncaged. Root faked right, faked left, and then, after a nanosecond of hope, was torpedoed onto his back.

The hit had a sickening sound to it, like a 50-pound sack of sugar being dropped from a two-story roof. But the sound of the hit was quickly replaced by the sound of Ricky Root's half-moan, half-scream.

The football had popped loose, though nobody bothered to retrieve it. Players in both lines stood wide-eyed, waiting to assess the carnage. John Nordyke got up off the ground. Ricky Root did not.

Instead, he laid there on his back, writhing in pain. One of his legs was pinned back in a discombobulated position, like that of a rag doll tossed from the top of a bunk bed.

"Quick," somebody said, "call an ambulance."

When it arrived, it drove right onto the practice field. The EMTs took off Ricky's helmet and carefully placed him on a stretcher. And just like that, he was gone.

I never played organized football after that year; neither, to my knowledge, did Ricky Root. He never said anything to me about the incident, nor I to him.

I saw him on and off in high school. He was what we called a "hard guy," a "parking lot" guy. He wore a leather jacket and smoked. His photo never appeared in my three annuals; his name wasn't among the Class of '72 graduates. He never made it to any class reunions.

From time to time, I wonder what happened to Ricky Root — and if the meat grinder incident made what may have been a tough life for him even tougher. From time to time, I think we all look back with regret at things we did or didn't do, incidents in which we never intended for someone to get hurt but they did anyway.

Someone told me he'd died in a car accident, something I haven't been able to confirm.

Years ago, I created a file — "Root, Ricky" — and stowed away some phone numbers that might have been his — just in case I ever found the courage to say I was sorry. But as with many of life's would-be apologies, it appears I've waited too long to find that courage.

Because, beyond the yard lines, there's not always a "next year" to wait for.

Ashes and dust

Jennie, Jennie, you've got to understand. I believe that God made me for a purpose. For China. But He also made me fast, and when I run I feel His pleasure. To give it up would be to hold Him in contempt.
— Eric Liddell in *Chariots of Fire*

When seeing me run cross-country in high school, I'm not sure if God felt pleasure or if He just winced; I was no Eric Liddell, a gold medal winner in the 1924 Olympics who went on to become a missionary in China. But my days as a competitive runner taught me life lessons that I still lean on three decades later: To push myself to the limits. To endure even when it hurts and I'm far behind the leaders. And to only run in Doberman-free zones.

I fell in love with running accidentally on purpose. The accidental part was that when I turned out for eighth-grade track, the coaches relegated me to the 1320 (three-lap) event because I was too slow, weak and un-springy for anything else. The on-purpose part was that, as a ninth-grader, I saw All-American runner Steve Prefontaine of Coos Bay, Oregon, set a national two-mile record on the very Corvallis High track on which I would train the next fall if I ran cross-country.

So I turned out for the team. Not because, like the woman touching the robe of Jesus, I thought running on the same track as "Pre" would miraculously heal me of my distance-running deficiencies. But because watching Prefontaine run awakened something deep inside me. I was drawn by the simplicity of a sport that was basically man vs. time. I was drawn by the proverbial loneliness of the long-distance runner; you either succeeded or failed all on your own. And I was drawn by the realization that for a 125-pound kid who would rather eat raw Brussels sprouts for a week than wrestle, running was my last best hope to stay involved in sports.

Unlike Prefontaine, I did not set my sights on a national record. My goal was much less lofty: to someday run in the Oregon state Class AAA cross-country meet. Pre had won the event as a junior and senior; I just wanted to be invited to the party. It became my quiet crusade.

I could qualify for the state cross-country race in one of two ways: by finishing as one of the top seven individuals in the district meet or by being on one of the top two teams. I ran JV as a sophomore. I didn't make it as a junior on varsity; neither did the team. Thus, I had one last chance to make state — my senior year.

Because of teammates graduating, moving and suffering collapsed lungs because of overzealous trumpet blowing, I suddenly found myself going into the summer before that year as Corvallis High's top runner. It was like one of those disaster movies in which, after the plane crashes, the entire flight crew dies and some nerd gets appointed leader because he once earned a Cub Scouts Wolf Badge for successfully making bread-on-a-stick.

But I had three months to prepare for the start of the season, and I vowed to simply be the best runner I could be. My opening workout, May 24, 1971, wasn't particularly promising:

> Jog 440. 3-mile all out in 19:02. Muscles didn't hurt. Stomach did. Barfed.

June 3's entry wasn't much more encouraging.

> Ran 3 miles to Skyline West before a dog bit me and I got lost. Disappointing workout. I'll bounce back.

And I did. After summer days of raking green beans onto a conveyor belt at a cannery, I would ride my bicycle three miles home, change into my running gear and be off.

Almost always by myself, I ran the country roads around Corvallis, into McDonald Forest, to the top of Ivy Hill. I ran carefully selected routes that took me by the houses of girls who, I always hoped, would be gazing out their windows, awaiting their knight in Property of CHS armor. (No such luck.) I ran to Oregon State's track and did timed laps. I ran stadium stairs. On family vacations, I ran at the beach and on hiking trails high in the Cascade Mountains. I ran all-comers meets every few weeks to test myself.

Each workout became a test, a challenge, a step that would reward me in the cool of autumn, when I'd be trying to pass some South Salem runner in Avery Park. As I pounded my way up Norwood Hill and headed for the telephone-pole finish line in front of my house, I'd imagine it to be the final 100 yards of the district cross-country race.

I'd glance at my hand-held stopwatch and if it read, say, 57:17, I'd pretend that I had to beat 57:30 to finish seventh and make it to state. Then, just like Pre, I'd kick into overdrive, as a small crowd — say, Mrs. Rudinsky, raking her lawn, and my dad, sanding a boat in our driveway — turned and looked. Chest burning and knees pumping, I headed for the finish line.

I charted every workout on the backs of order forms used by my father's photography business. I meticulously kept track of every mile run — 639 1/2 as a junior and 744 as a senior, a combined amount, I later figured, that would get me from Seattle to L.A. I also rated each workout, four dots for an outstanding effort and one dot for poor.

I gave myself four dots for a workout on July 17 — because I ran a marathon. These were the days before marathons meant 10,000 people oozing across the Brooklyn Bridge in New York City. Before people realized that it might not be a smart idea to hold a 26-mile race in the dead of summer, particularly one starting as late as 9 a.m. on an 85-degree day, as this one did.

After running for 22 miles, getting a drink at a farmhouse, walking three miles, then plodding the final mile, I finished. I remember seeing the end of the 1968 Olympic Marathon in Mexico City on TV, the runners triumphantly entering the stadium to the cheers of 80,000 people. When I arrived at Newberg High — photos don't lie — exactly seven people were on hand: three other runners, three meet officials, and a former Corvallis runner named Ted Wolfe, who was my ride home.

A young woman behind a card table handed me a certificate that said "Berrian Festival Marathan 1971" — yep, marathon was misspelled. I finished in four hours, 19 minutes and 25.4 seconds. But that was good enough for tenth place! That night, I wrote in my journal: "I must admit, I'm inspired."

While raking beans each day at the cannery, I daydreamed about the state cross-country meet and, more immediately, about breaking 5 minutes in the mile. I had broken 5:10 half a dozen times, even run 5:00.0, but never been officially below the Bannister-plus-a-minute barrier. Later that summer, I did it in an all-comers meet.

> This may sound stupid a long time from now, but I'm happy. 4:59.8. I won! I like the feeling of winning.

I had once won a 440-yard race at an all-comers meet because the only other runner was a shot-putter trying to get in shape for football. But my win in the mile was the first time I'd ever won a distance race of any sort. It would also be my last.

Two days later I ran a steeplechase race and an all-out 440 at an all-comers race. "Leg sore," I reported in the journal. By Sept. 10, I couldn't run. Period.

I had shin splints in one of my legs. I'd overrun. Too many miles. Too little rest. My season, the doctor said, was probably over. It couldn't be over, I told him; I was a senior. I needed to run at district so I could qualify for state.

My coach put me on a swimming and weight lifting program with hopes that I might be ready to run one dual meet, then district. On October 14, I toed the line for my first competitive race in more than a month. I had trained little, but somehow felt that I could run strong. I was wrong. I finished 17th out of 17.

But my journal suggested I wasn't quitting.

> Oddly enough, I'm confident for district. I'm just going to make up my mind and go when it hurts. I'm going to kill myself but I'm going to run well.

My state-meet dream died in a driving rainstorm. I finished 34th, 27 places behind what I needed to qualify for state. The team finished third. Nobody from Corvallis High was going to state. The season was over. My high school career was over.

Afterward, I thought back to those hot summer nights, chugging up Norwood Hill to finish yet another workout, buoyed by whatever challenge I had made for myself and met. Now I sat in an cold bus, raindrops slaloming way down the windows, teammates filing past me and, I supposed, thinking that I'd failed them, the school, perhaps all of Western Civilization.

I've thought a lot about that season in the years since: how hard I had worked and how, in the end, all those miles and side aches — all that sweat and sacrifice — seemed to be for naught, a season summed up in a silly graph I created on a sheet of notebook paper: "How Shin Splits Affected Me," my miles-per-week looking so impressive, then plummeting like the Crash of '29.

What I've realized is that the experience was all for naught only if I believe value is limited to outcome, not process. It was for naught only if I believe value is limited to what the world allows us to qualify for — be it a record, a medal, or an invitation to a state cross-country meet, and not God's deeper purpose. It was for naught only if I failed to realize that some of life's best lessons are learned not through achieving but in simply trying.

God did not make me fast, like Liddell and Pre, but He did make me for a purpose, and I'm convinced that every mile I ran that summer had meaning to it. Every mile meant something beyond a scrawled line in my journal. Every mile was some sort of piece in the puzzle of who I would eventually become and how I would react when life as an adult got painful and when I realized I was far behind the leaders and when I simply wanted to quit, but did not.

Author Jack London, whose stories often examined man's courage to survive in a Yukon environment much harsher than a small-town high school's, once wrote that:

> I would rather be ashes than dust! I would rather that spark should burn out in a brilliant blaze than it should be stilled by dry rot .... The proper function of man is to live, not to exist. I shall not waste my days trying to prolong them. I shall use my time.

Man vs. time. More than 30 years have passed since those summer evenings when I'd pound up Norwood Hill, and I'm still running. A few years back, I ran another marathon, at 41. I've run in the largest running-relay in the world, the Hood to Coast. I've run in the deep heat of the South, in the deep snows of Central Oregon. I've run along Canada's Lake Ontario, at dawn high above the Grand Canyon, on rutted roads in Haiti with a dozen barefoot children gleefully following my every step. Don't get me wrong; I'm still a hack. But

I still run.

Just a few days ago, I was finishing an early-morning run on an Oregon beach when, just before Starr Creek, about 200 yards from the rocks I call my finish line, I glanced at my wristwatch: 49:19.

Instinctively, I kicked into overdrive. I splashed through the creek — the coastal answer to the steeplechase —while a couple of curious beachcombers looked up from their shell-searching to watch. What they saw, I suppose, was mid-life madness. What I saw was something else: the finish line of a cross-country course. And if I could break 50 minutes, a chance to finish seventh.

And make it to state.

America

I met him at our neighborhood Fourth of July barbecue in Bellevue, Washington. The host had each of us stand and tell something about ourselves. We told of our jobs, our families, our hobbies — the usual stuff.

Then it was his turn, the stocky man with the thick mustache and the strange accent who lived next door to us in Bellevue, Washington. He told of his job, his family, his hobbies — the usual stuff.

"And," said Boris Moskalensky, "I'm proud to be an American."

I had seen plenty of Fourth of July barbecues before. I had seen all the trappings — flags and fireworks, burgers and baseball. But until that moment, I had never seen anyone stand up and say he was proud to be an American.

On Independence Day 1988, the neighbors in our cul-de-sac taught Boris Moskalensky how to play baseball and slap a high-five. And Boris Moskalensky taught us how to appreciate something that many of us had taken for granted: a place called America.

The difference between Boris and his neighbors was clear. We had never known the flipside to the independence we so casually celebrated. But Boris had lived under communist rule for 42 years. Until coming to America, he had never known the freedom he had come to embrace so fervently.

He told us that people growing up in American didn't understand what it's like not to be free. He told us he knew the difference because, as he put it, he had spent 42 years in jail. Or running from those who wanted him in jail.

As we gathered round, he told stories of the Hungarian Revolution in 1956. Of working for the Soviet military. Of seeing trainloads of wounded soldiers returning from battle. And of thinking, for the first time, that his country was evil.

The Hungarians, he said, just wanted a new way to live. They were not fascists. They were just people looking for something better than they had. As were Boris and his family in the years to come.

He began questioning his country more and more. He began listening to American broadcasts on short-wave radio and realized there was another way to live. He realized he lived in a country that regularly lied to him.

In the late '70s, the Soviets loosened their emigration policy and Boris made his decision: He and his family would try to come to America. Word got out. His wife was fired from her job as a chemistry lab assistant. His son, a top student, was kicked out of school; the authorities said the boy was the son of a traitor.

Finally, the papers came. Permission was granted. But two weeks before they were to leave, Boris and Susana were confronted by two men who began bad-mouthing his wife. Boris readied his fists, but he knew the trap. Knew who they were: The KGB. Knew the stories of how they would instigate a fight, throw the husband in jail for assault and leave him there for years, snuffing any dreams of departing for a better place.

But Boris refused to give up on that dream. Finally, after much more waiting and worrying, they were given clearance to leave. They moved to Seattle. What they found was the fresh air of freedom — and people who took much for granted.

He found it unbelievable that, just from studying for his citizenship test, he knew more about the country's history than many Americans who were born here.

He found it unbelievable that an election might draw only half of all registered voters.

He found it unbelievable that the country spends so much on welfare. Once, when the auto store Boris worked at went out of business, friends told him to go on welfare. He refused. I didn't do anything for this country, he said, why should they feel obligated to do something for me?

During the Olympic Games, people asked him if it was hard to decide who he wanted to win. Not at all, he would tell them. Russia is a country, he would say. The United States is *my* country.

You want to know the difference between the Soviet Union and America, he asked. Watch when they raise the flag for the Olympic champions. The Americans will have tears in their eyes, he said, because they are proud of their country. The Russians will not, because winning to them means only a better life. A job. But not pride for their country.

After the barbecue, as dusk descended, the folks in the neighborhood took to the middle of the cul-de-sac for a game of baseball. Boris had never played the game before and we taught him to field, bat and speak "infield" — "hey, batta, batta, hey, batta, batta, swing!"

I will never forget what happened the first time he stepped to the plate. He swung mightily time after time after time. Nothing but air. Finally, he connected, a dribbler back to the pitcher. Boris dropped his bat and started running. He was out at first but seemed oblivious to that reality. Instead, he rounded first, raced to second and headed for third.

My goodness, I realized: We had forgotten to teach him about running the bases and what constitutes an out. At first we hooted and hollered and politely pointed out that he was out, but Boris kept chugging, so we all just stopped shouting and eagerly watched. And smiled.

Boris rounded third and headed for the plate. He had a huge smile on his face, like a man who had been running his whole life and was finally coming home.

Underdogs

On a November night in 1994, while shooting hoops in the dark with my then-15-year-old son Ryan, I said it. Only hours earlier, the University of Oregon's football team, picked to finish near the bottom of the Pac-10 that year, had clinched a spot in the Rose Bowl, which would be the school's first trip to Pasadena since seemingly the days when dinosaurs were halftime entertainment. As the hot-off-the-press shirts would say in the next few days: "Just Like Clockwork— Every 37 Years Oregon Goes to the Rose Bowl." We hadn't been since 1958. At the time, I was 4 years old.

"Ryan," I said. "Enjoy this. Because it will never, ever get better than this."

I believed it then. I believe it now. Nothing beats winning when you're not expected to win. Nothing beats knocking the unbelievers on their keisters. Nothing beats overachieving as an underdog.

I once watched a vacation-riddled Kidsports baseball team, fielding only seven players, go the distance against a nine-man team in a championship game that had a little bit of everything, including an automatic sprinkler system turning on because the game had gone so deep into the night. The team lost 10-9 in the last inning, but I still consider South Eugene's effort that night — their catcher was pitching, having never thrown a game until that night, and one of the seven could only bunt because of a sore shoulder — one of the most heroic sports efforts I've ever witnessed.

Why do we love the upset? Because when Oregon State's 1985 football team beats the University of Washington as a 37-point underdog (See "The Impossible Dream," Page 197) we file that away for a day when we find ourselves as 37-point underdogs in life.

Because it reminds us, as Hebrews says, that "faith is being sure of what we hope for and certain of what we do not see."

Because it helps us believe — if not in the impossible dream then at least some kind of dream, which is the biggest hurdle for underdogs: not to overcome whatever odds the opposition presents, but to overcome ourselves. Our doubts. Our fears.

Early '60s. My pal Mike Larkin's parents were gone and, in his house down the street from mine in Corvallis, he opened the drawer and gently pulled it out: The Bellfountain High basketball uniform. He held it up as if it were no less holy than the ark of the covenant.

It was a ragged black singlet with orange piping and numerals. No. 5. And shiny black pants to match.

"My dad played for this little school that won the state basketball championship," Mike told me.

Not just any state championship basketball team, you later learn. The most phenomenal basketball team in the history of the state. In 1937, David smote Goliath in Oregon's version of *Hoosiers*.

Bellfountain, a school of 27 total students, beat Franklin of Portland, (2,100 students) in the state semifinals, then Lincoln of Portland (1,728 students) in the finals.

Bellfountain sits about five miles northwest of Monroe in Oregon's Willamette Valley. In the '30s, it was a blink-and-you'll-miss-it town where nearly everyone was a logger, millworker or farmer.

In earlier years, Bellfountain lit its gym for games by having fans pull their Model T's in front of open doors and turning on their headlights.

In 1936, Bellfountain finished third in the state. The next year, the "Bells" as they were called, proved they were no fluke. At the 1937 state tournament at Willamette High in Salem, Bellfountain beat Amity and Chiloquin to claim the Class B championship, then Franklin in the semifinals of the overall tournament.

That set up the title game, the first time a "B" school had ever made it to the finals. "Go get 'em," read a telegram from Corvallis High students, whose team had been beaten by the Bells. "We are here for you, 600 strong."

Bellfountain beat Lincoln for the championship, 35-21. Fans rushed the court. Headlines around the state knighted the team as "Giant Killers." Players and coaches were feted at banquets.

A year later, Bellfountain High consolidated with nearby Monroe. Only one player went on to college. Most went to war. One, John Key, was killed on Okinawa.

Because Oregon, like other states, is now broken into numerous classifications, such an upset can never happen again, a school with 27 students beating schools with 1,700-plus. But it happened once. In 1937. In a place that now exists only in the minds of those few of us privileged to know the story.

When such underdogs overcome, they inspire those around them. When some team or individual does what seems impossible, it's like the POW soldiers who beats the odds to escape. It gives the rest of the prisoners the one thing that's keeping them alive: hope.

Because we tend to be slaves to the expectations of others. A child abused when young is more likely to grow up to be an abuser than a child who is not. A child given the freedom to soar when young is more likely to grow up and soar. The underdogs have it tougher. They must persevere against a world that says: *You can't.*

Katey Gries was a 46-year-old student of mine in a reporting class I taught at the University of Oregon. A high school dropout who had been preyed upon by an alcoholic stepfather. Who had gotten into drugs and began hooking up with one loser after another. Who was raped at 22.

The message people kept giving her was this: You're worthless. You're nobody. You're here to be used by the cowardly losers who, lacking the courage to beat their own odds, prey on anyone they recognize as weaker than themselves. And their preying reinforces the feeling of worthlessness in those preyed-upon.

Which is why Gries feared everything and everyone around her. She slept with .357-Magnum under her bed. She drank. "I remember thinking: 'You're never going to amount to anything,' " she says.

We live in an instant age, an age when we can zap our dinner in a minute, download a song on our iPods in the clicks of a few buttons, find the score of any game in the country in only seconds. And so, of course, we've come to believe that underdogs — as the movies would have us believe — can bounce back in the blink of an eye.

No. It takes time. It took years for Gries to learn she had value. Years to learn to quit clinging to losers. Years to work through a "Turning Point" program at Lane Community College and wind up in my classroom, surrounded, frankly, by a lot of 20-something students who'd been raised as "favored ones."

She emerged as my best student. She made the Dean's List, posted a 3.66 GPA and was inducted into the invitation-only Kappa Tau Alpha national honor society. All while being a single mom, working in the dining room of a nursing home to pay for college and volunteering for an organization that helps battered women.

She won a prestigious scholarship. And landed a yearlong internship with the UO's alumni magazine.

Why? Because she finally quit listening to the others and began listening to something deep within, that flicker of hope that the world tries to quench — and usually does, frankly — but she refused to let die.

It has been 12 years since the night I told Ryan to enjoy this feeling because it would never get better. Oregon has enjoyed some great football success in those 12 years. But, then, the more you win, the more you're expected to win and the less each win means. Because winning while hungry means more than winning while full. "You may glory in a team triumphant, but you fall in love with a team in defeat," Roger Kahn writes in *The Boys of Summer*.

After the Ducks' Rose Bowl year, some fans became cocky. Some groused over winning seasons that, only a decade ago, they would have loved to have. Some came to believe that the team owed them.

In 2001, seven years after its Rose Bowl year, Oregon finished second in the country with a lopsided win over Colorado in the Fiesta Bowl. I remember, after filing a column from the press box in Tempe, Arizona, standing high up in the stadium and thinking what a great feeling it is to win. I called Ryan back in Oregon on my cell phone and we shared our exhilaration.

It was sweet. But, as I'd said on that November night long before, not quite as sweet as it would ever be again.

Rental clubs

I could barely hear the voice on the other end of the long-distance call. "Dad," said my 19-year-old son Ryan, "I just played the worst two rounds of golf since I was a sophomore in high school."

Along with his college golf team, he had entered this out-of-state tournament with great expectations. With just a single round left to play, he now had no expectations. He was so disappointed he could barely talk, much less motivate himself to bounce back.

He was the two-time champion of our city's only 18-hole public course. As a freshman, he shot a final-round 69 to win the conference's fall championship. But on this rainy April day, 18 months later, he had shot 94 and 93, scores usually reserved for guys like me.

"I am one bad golfer," he said.

"Ry, you're a great golfer who had one bad day," I said.

What made it worse was that his cousin Brad, who lived nearby but had never seen him play, had followed him around.

"I'm so embarrassed," Ryan said.

Perhaps you know what it's like to be a parent in a situation like this. You want to say something profound, something emotionally invigorating, something that will instill hope in a child of yours who has none. But the more you talk, the more you realize how uninspiring you are. The "tomorrow-will-be-another-day" stuff doesn't cut it with a kid who has just made more double bogeys in a day than he usually makes in a season.

Still, sometimes when we open the refrigerator of our minds, all we find is leftovers. I reached behind the mayonnaise for the two-day-old pizza wrapped in aluminum foil.

"Hey," I said. "Tomorrow's another day. Forget what happened today. Go out there, remember who you are, remember what you've done in the past and have fun."

I heard this slight half groan on the other end of the line, like someone waking up after gall bladder surgery.

"I'll be praying for you, buddy," I said.

For Ryan, the next day dawned a lot like the previous day: rainy. The coach drove the team from the motel to the course. Ryan was standing outside the van, talking with his cousin-the-masochist — back for the final round despite having seen the first two — and turned to get his clubs.

That's when he noticed his coach was driving out of the club's parking lot — with Ryan's clubs still inside. All the other players had gotten theirs except for him.

Ryan figured the coach was just going to get a quick cup of coffee. But about 45 minutes before his tee time, Ryan asked a teammate where the coach had gone.

"To a tire shop to get the spare fixed."

Gulp.

Ryan's cousin had a car. The two of them jumped in and started frantically scouring the streets of Olympia, Washington, looking for a white van on a garage hoist. No luck. They stopped and asked directions to the nearest tire shop and found it, but the coach wasn't there. They headed back to the golf course. No van. No coach. No clubs.

"Next up on the tee," said a voice on the loudspeaker, "the three-some of Ryan Welch of Linfield College ..."

Tournament golf, you may know, is a game of precise rules, one of which says that if you aren't able to hit your ball when it's your turn to tee off, you're toast. DQ'd. Disqualified.

Instincts kicked in. Ryan raced into the pro shop and spewed his dilemma. A pro shop attendant responded like a good EMT, throwing together a bag of rental clubs to stabilize this young man's life until the ambulance — a white van with a set of golf clubs inside — could arrive on the scene.

At one point, the bag had a left-handed seven-iron in it; Ryan isn't left-handed. The final concoction looked like this: 10 clubs (you're allowed 14), including a crooked putter and a demo driver that, says Ryan, "was like swinging a shovel."

A teammate handed him a handful of well-beaten balls. Despite slick conditions, he was forced to wear a pair of running shoes, not golf spikes.

It wasn't a pretty start. He double bogeyed the first two holes, a pace that had him on target for 108, and set up the kind of moment that, in our family, reminds us all of the scene in the movie *Trading Places* when Dan Akroyd — a once-wealthy man who had the world at his fingertips — finds himself standing on the sidewalk in the rain, dressed as Santa Claus, his beard matted with fried chicken. What, he wonders, could possibly be worse than this?

Slowly, Akroyd looks down and sees what could be worse than this: A dog has mistaken his leg for a fire hydrant.

But no dog came sniffing Ry's golf shoes on this soggy morning. Instead, on the third hole, he rolled in a 12-foot birdie — his first of the tournament. On the fifth hole, he drained a 50-foot birdie.

He suddenly had new hope, a new attitude and a red-hot rental putter.

He continued to play solid, and sometimes spectacular, golf. On the 18th hole, after scuffing the shovel driver 75 yards off the tee, he scrambled to within 8 feet of the hole, sank a putt and posted a 79. He had played the final 16 holes in just three over par, posted the best score on the team, and finished among the top 10 for the day.

I often tell this story at men's retreats because I believe it says something about life and circumstances and how we react to those circumstances. On my wall hangs a tattered quote from Chuck Swindoll:

> We cannot change our past. We cannot change the fact that people will act in a certain way. We cannot change the inevitable. The only thing we can do is play on the one string we have, and that is our attitude. I am convinced that life is 10 percent what happens to me and 90 percent how I react to it.

Ryan didn't get to choose what clubs he played with on this particular day. But he did have a say in how he was going to respond to that situation. Low as he was, he somehow mustered what little hope he had to not only weather the storm, but to rise above it.

Beyond the golf course, life sometimes swirls with much stiffer challenges. Ryan's cousin, Brad, who tromped 54 holes with his pal in the rain and mud over those two days, couldn't stop his younger brother from falling into an icy river and dying on the last day of 1994. But he did have a say in how he was going to respond to that tragedy, and he courageously chose to not give up on life or God or himself in the years that followed.

A young man at a men's retreat I was leading couldn't stop his father from committing suicide when the boy was only 5 years old. But he did have a say in how he was going to respond to that tragedy — and now is a committed father, husband, and a follower of God who is intent on starting a new legacy for his own son.

After I told the story of Ryan's golf comeback, I asked the men at that retreat if anyone could relate with their own lives — lives whose obstacles were far more treacherous than sand traps and split-level greens.

Men are often reluctant to share from their hearts, but the man whose father had killed himself stood up and began his story with a line I will never forget.

"You might say life gave me the rental clubs," he said.

But the triumph of his testimony — and of all those who rise above the circumstances — is in an attitude that says the strength inside me can overcome whatever's outside me.

It's an attitude that says I'll trust God even when I don't understand why my clubs weren't there for me.

It's not looking back, not even ahead, but looking up — "from whence my strength cometh," says Isaiah.

It's playing those rental clubs for all they're worth, which is a lot when in the hands of a faithful follower.

We live by encouragement and die without it
— slowly, sadly, angrily.

— Celeste Holm

3

The
Coach

A 1990 photo of the author with his Camp Creek Beavers reflects the levity sports can breed. Years later, though, he'd anguish after learning one player was headed for prison. (Sally Welch)

First season

In every coach's memory, there lives a first season. Mine unfolded when I was 23 years old. I can't remember why I agreed to coach baseball — temporary insanity comes to mind — but I was handed a rag-tag group of fifth-graders formed by taking the stragglers from the league's six other teams. It was like trying to decorate your living room with garage-sale items that hadn't sold by noon.

The only thing we had less of than talent was confidence. "Coach," said one boy while warming up at our first practice, "I think we're going to lose a lot this year."

"But how can you say that?" I said. "You haven't even seen the other players yet. We're an expansion team, sure, but we might be good."

"It's just a feeling I have," he said.

The kid turned out to be a good hitter and a good fielder. But his greatest gift, I soon found, was prophecy; he could correctly predict the future.

We lost a lot. We lost our first two games by a combined score of — I'm not kidding here — 60-0. Over the season, we lost by an average score of 20-4.

Despite such lopsided games, I will never forget that first season, snippets of which I offer here, culled from a journal I kept during the nine weeks:

May 5. I never realized 11- and 12-year-olds asked so many questions:

"Where's the bathroom?"

"What color will our uniforms be?"

"When is the first game?"

"Why is the field so bumpy?"

"Why is there only one bat?"

"What kind of mileage does your Datsun B-210 get?"

One kid wanted to know if we could have Farrah Fawcett-Majors iron-ons to decorate the back of our jerseys.

The Prophet may be right: We might lose a lot. It's just a feeling I have.

May 12. Our catcher is the biggest character on the team. He's not much larger than a 32-ounce bat and has never caught before. The equipment hangs on him like a Charlie Brown Christmas tree with oversized ornaments.

He's a feisty, mischievous kid, a Dennis-the-Menace type who says what's on his mind. After he muffed a play, I gave him two laps today for saying what was on his mind. But for some reason I can't help but like the guy.

May 19. Our first game was one of those good news/bad news events. The good news: Our pitcher threw a no-hitter. The bad news: We lost 7-3. Control is not his forte. He walked 13 batters.

May 24. Our first pitcher walked eight batters and we fell behind 10-0 after the first inning. (We had only one out at that point but the ump ended the inning because of the 10-run rule.)

The catcher went out to the mound to discuss things with the pitcher. When the meeting was over, the pitcher looked shaken. After the inning was over, the shortstop came to me.

"Coach," he said, "you'd better do something about our catcher."

Our catcher? Wouldn't it be more appropriate to do something about our pitcher, the guy who kept giving opponents the get-on-base-free cards?

"Our catcher?" I asked.

"Yeah, he came out to the mound and told Billy he was going to punch him in the nose if he didn't start throwing strikes."

The game was called after three innings. We lost 33-0. Tonight I found myself checking the schedule to see when our last game is. I circled it on my calendar, the way you would circle Christmas or a vacation or something else that couldn't come soon enough.

May 31. After losing 27-0 and 13-2, the team's morale has begun to sink. The players don't mind losing. It's losing without uniforms that bothers them so much. In addition, they wish they could have a jug of Kool-Aid on the bench like other teams.

June 6. The uniforms arrive. I'm hoping the additional team pride will help us play better.

June 7. I think I hoped for the impossible. We lost 21-0 today. But I must admit, we looked sharp doing so. And were rarely thirsty on our journey to defeat. We have Kool-Aid now.

Our catcher, I've noticed, carries on a running conversation with the plate umpire, the batter, and, sometimes, the fans. Today the umpire politely told him that if the kid spoke again, he would drop-kick the young man over second base. For the first time, he shut up.

June 20. Our losing streak has increased to seven games. I was putting away the gear after today's 25-3 loss when a little boy who had apparently watched the game rolled up on his bicycle.

"Mister, are you the coach of that team that lost today?" he said.

"I sure am," I said, half-expecting a word of encouragement.

"That's too bad," he said and rode away.

July 5. We're getting better. An umpire today told me we were the most improved team in the league. We've dropped 12 straight now.

I've made some coaching errors and the kids have made some playing errors, but our fans have remained loyal — even the shortstop's mom, who has to keep the scorebook for games like our 33-0 loss that involved 23 errors and 41 stolen bases. It is a herculean task, like keeping minutes at a school board meeting that turns into a brawl.

A team with a 19-1 lead stole home on us. An old season is getting older.

Right now, our magic number is eight: Eight more days until the season is over. Two more games. Tomorrow's is against the other expansion team, the only team in the league that we've held to fewer than 13 runs.

"How many of you think we can win tomorrow?" I asked at the end of practice. Every player's hand shot up without hesitation. I didn't know whether to laugh or cry.

July 6. Today I laughed. We all laughed. Because we did it. We finally won a game. Coaches are never supposed to show a lack of confidence. They're supposed to say things like "never say die" and "winners never quit and quitters never win." But as we took the field in the bottom of the last inning with an 8-6 lead, I was the "ye of little faith" poster boy.

I was scared. Scared because in 59 innings during the season, only six times had we held our opponents to less than two runs. One in 10 odds. But now, that's what we had to do to win.

What happened next was something that hadn't happened all season. Our pitcher, Brian, struck out all three batters. Just like that. As if he'd done it all season long.

For an instant, I just stood there like a caged animal set free, not knowing quite what to do, having never known what freedom was.

Some of the players leaped for joy. The shortstop had tears in his eyes. I joined in the celebration, which shifted to the A&W when the first baseman's father said the drinks were on him.

Our catcher took a long pull on his root beer, then looked over at me. "Hey coach," he said, his face smudged with dirt from the mask, "we finally winned one."

"Yeah, we did," I said. "We winned one."

It was the lead item in the Little League baseball roundup the next day in our town's newspaper. That's not too surprising, considering I was the sports editor of that paper and wrote the article myself, though I did have the ethical tact to not interview and quote myself.

July 13. In the final game of the season, our winning streak was halted at one. But, oh, what a winning streak it was: short, but like any time in life when we find the light after a long period of darkness, so very, very sweet.

Old gray-haired guy

Someone once asked me who I thought was the best coach I'd ever had the privilege to watch. I thought of John Wooden, who coached UCLA basketball teams to a record 10 NCAA titles in 12 years. I thought of Don Shula, the ex-Miami Dolphins coach who won more games than anyone in NFL history. I thought of four-time NCAA Football Coach-of-the Year Joe Paterno of Penn State, who's won more college football games than anybody still coaching.

Then I thought of Steve Panter, a guy so obscure some of his neighbors probably don't even know him. Each November for more than two decades, as the winter rains descend on Oregon, he pulls out a bag of basketballs from the trunk of his car, grabs his clipboard and ice pack, and walks into a middle-school gym whose door is always propped open by a rug, lest it lock.

Like thousands of other men and women across the country, Steve Panter coaches kids. But what separates him from so many is exactly that: He coaches kids. He doesn't use kids to fuel his selfish dreams. He doesn't turn kids into robo-warriors. He doesn't berate kids.

He teaches. He inspires. He leads. And does so with more compassion than anyone I've ever seen.

Now 50-plus and a grandfather, he calls himself "the old gray-haired guy," though racquetball and road biking keep him in solid shape. For most of his coaching career, he's taken the same eighth-grade team — not the top-level players; instead, the ones who hoped to make the top team but didn't. He puts in about three months a year, four or five days a week. For that, he gets a five-dollars-off coupon for his child to play in the league, which is of little use since his two sons are grown.

His teams have made it to the city finals six times and claimed a city championship, so he knows how to win. But the true measure of a coach isn't found in city championships or in victories. It's not even found under the glare of gymnasium lights. Instead, it's found in the bond — or lack thereof — between coach and players.

• It's found in a dim-lit hallway when a lanky forward slumped against the wall in anguish, having just missed a handful of lay-ins that would have sealed a championship game. Instead, Panter's team lost by a point.

In the gym, the victors celebrated with gusto. Panter's team, meanwhile, wandered around like jet-crash victims, having been ahead by seven points with less than two minutes to go before their dream crashed and burned.

In such situations, I've seen losing coaches slam down clipboards. I've seen coaches speed-walk, head down, to the locker room. I've seen coaches verbally pounce on referees. But what I saw this Sunday afternoon was a coach notice a lone player in a hallway in tears.

I saw that coach put his arm around the young man, smile and console him with words that did not come easy — I know Panter was hurting, too — but nevertheless came: Words that affirmed the players. " ... without you, we never would have gotten close to the finals ..." Words that encouraged. " ... hurts now but trials like this will toughen you ..." Words that enlightened: " ... life is way more important than a basketball game ... ."

• It's found behind the school, where one of Panter's players had left a practice after a run-in with some teammates. Panter ran after the kid. He knew the general situation: The boy's parents were getting divorced and the kid had been handed off to grandparents. There was a sadness about him.

Panter asked the boy why he was leaving. "Neither of my parents want me," he said. "I'm living with my grandparents, and they don't want me either. Now some of the kids on the team just told me they don't want me. In the whole world, nobody wants me. I don't belong anywhere."

Panter knelt down and searched for words. The kid sobbed on his shoulder. Finally, the words just came: "John, I know a place where you belong — right here. I'm your coach and I want you on my team."

He remembers two things about what he told the kid: first, that the words seemed to have come down from On High — "What do you say to a kid in such despair?" — and, second, that they seemed to instantaneously ease the kid's pain.

Panter and the boy walked back to the team, which was practicing with an assistant coach. Panter stopped practice, gathered the players together and explained what teams were all about: Togetherness. Respect. Forgiveness. "Everyone earned a spot on this team," he said. "Everyone belongs."

• It's found on a high school stage where a handful of seniors were being asked questions as part of a variety-show fundraiser.

One of the contestants was a "Panter kid" who had grown to nearly seven feet tall. Though six-foot-three even as an eighth grader, when he played for Panter he was too lazy to use his height. He wouldn't go to the hoop, wouldn't establish his presence, wouldn't be aggressive.

Once during practice, with Panter playing on the defensive team, the boy put up his usual lazy shot. The coach, 5-foot-11, leaped high, and blocked it with both hands. The boy fell on his back, more surprised than hurt.

From that point on, the kid became a basketball player. By late in his senior year of high school, he was among the league's best players. He also had among the league's hottest tempers, had gotten a few technical fouls and had been suspended for a game.

About then, he ran into his old coach.

"What's going on?" Panter asked.

The player tried to rationalize his behavior. But just as he had five years ago, Panter blocked the shot with a verbal challenge. Didn't he remember what the old gray-haired guy had told him about how losing your temper on the court was an advantage to the opposition? About how it takes energy away from your game? About how life isn't always fair, and neither are some calls, but you can't waste your time complaining?

From that point, the kid's attitude started improving. He won a college scholarship. And there he was, the spring of his senior year, up on the stage, as the contest host asked, "What one person has had the most influence on your life to this point?"

He thought for only a moment.

"My eighth-grade basketball coach," he said.

The old gray-haired guy was once a yeller and a screamer, he'll tell you, but the rafting accident in 1986 changed all that. Unconscious in the cold McKenzie River water for about five minutes — his head having hit a cooler or a rock — he'd come as close to death as he ever had. Before the accident, he'd known something was missing in his life; he saw this as an icy wakeup call. He began trusting God, not himself, and, over time, noticed his priorities changing from getting his way to giving to others, from winning games to nurturing kids.

For Panter, basketball is not life; it's a part of life, a way to learn about life. He doesn't humiliate players who have made mistakes with words that hurt; instead, he'll tell them, "You just had a stupid attack. That doesn't mean you're bad, it just means you did something wrong."

He looks for the positive. He minimizes running drills and maximizes basketball; "It's a game," he says. "That means it's supposed to be fun."

He honestly believes the " … how-you-play-the-game" axiom, and abhors a league rule that says if one team gets ahead of another by more than 15 points, the free-standing scoreboard must be turned around so spectators can't see.

"What that says to a coach and team is, 'You should be ashamed of yourselves. You're so bad we don't want people to see how much better the other team is than you.' Hogwash. If they're playing their hardest, that team should be proud of every point it gets. And what about that reserve who maybe gets his first basket of the season? Shouldn't he or she have the thrill of seeing those points be put on the board?"

He demands discipline: No swearing. No show boating. No failed classes. You play by the rules. You respect your opponent and the officials. And your coach and teammates.

But he leavens such demands with an allowance to be human. Sports are emotional, he'll tell his players; at times, you might feel like crying. So cry. Nothing to be ashamed of. Tears sometimes soothe the hurt.

He keeps his cool. In fact, the only time I've seen him flat-out mad was after a timekeeper clearly cheated so his son's team would have more time for a last-second shot to win — which is exactly what happened.

What incensed Panter wasn't that his team had lost, but that his players — kids — had been victimized by an adult who had ignored the rules of the game, who had sacrificed honor and fairness to the god of greed: winning.

Lots of coaches talk about their bottom lines being kids. Panter's truly is. He occasionally starts practices — after getting approval from parents — with a five-minute talk about attitude or drugs or sex. He takes his team each year to a youth detention center to show them where they might wind up if they make really bad choices. He has the courage to confront parents who push their kids too hard. He gives his MVP awards to every kid on the team.

He tells the players at the final banquet that they're welcome to call him, day or night, any hour, if they're ever in trouble, need help, or just want someone to listen. And more than one has taken him up on the offer.

The oldest Panter player is now about 30. Every now and then the coach will be at a restaurant or a game and he'll hear someone from behind say, "Hey, coach." And, more often than not, it will be a player who will not only reminisce about the old team but mention that he still has his MVP trophy or remembers that line about stupid attacks.

History will remember the Woodens, Shulas and Paternos of the world — and well it should. But kids who play sports will remember the Steve Panters of their childhoods, the coaches who, for a five-dollars-off coupon, teach not just the game of basketball or soccer or hockey, but the life stuff that lasts.

Wounded sparrows

Are not two sparrows sold for a penny? Yet not one of them will fall to the ground apart from the will of your Father. And even the very hairs of your head are all numbered. So don't be afraid; you are worth more than many sparrows.

— Matthew 10:29-31

The first basketball team I coached was at an elementary school so small that even when combining the fourth and fifth grades, I had to do some extensive recruiting just to have five starters. Camp Creek Elementary School outside Springfield had fewer students in its entire student body, 65, than my boys had had in their respective grades in the suburban school from which they'd transferred.

It was a bittersweet year. I recall walking out of the gym on a snowy night — rare for the rainy Willamette Valley — and driving slowly home on a country road with Ryan and Jason, thinking life doesn't get much better than being the first car on a snowy road after a good basketball practice with your two sons in back, talking about sledding the next day.

But I also recall learning that one of my players had a painful past. Shortly before the season, the father of one of my players had pulled his van off a country road one night, taken out a gun and shot himself in the head.

I realize this is a jolting image when juxtaposed beside pictures of snow-covered country roads, but the memory reminds me that, as coaches, the children we're charged with often arrive at practice with painful pasts — and painful presents — that we dare not ignore.

Whether we coach for a five-room country school or an urban youth league, we're responsible for children with baggage. Children who come from, and go back to, homes where hurt is a way of life. Children looking for something — even if they're not sure just what.

We may offer them a couple of hours of calm in lives that are otherwise catastrophic, stability in a sea of inconsistency, encouragement in a world where they get little. Once, at a coaches' clinic, the leader said something I will never forget: "As a coach, you may sometimes feel insignificant. But remember this: For some kids, you may be the only person all week who makes them feel like they're worth anything at all."

I wonder if some coaches understand what a crucial role they can play in the life of a child. I can think of a few coaches I've seen who did not, including the baseball coach who yanked his shortstop in mid-inning, right after the kid made an error; it was, he later said, "for the good of the team." Ten years later, when that humiliation still haunts the kid's subconscious, will it still seem like the best decision?

Some coaches underestimate how pivotal they can be in the lives of their players — not only in teaching them how to shoot a jump shot, but in how to believe in themselves. In how to be part of a team. In how to bounce back from defeat.

I look at my old team photos and I can still account for most of the kids, even though some of them are now more than six inches taller than me. In fact, after my last team broke up and the kids started high school, I wrote them each summer with a small word of encouragement, like a mother whose babe is heading off to camp for the first time. But a few come back Address Unknown.

News of them comes third-hand.

"Heard he moved to California to live with his father again."

"Someone said he was in the juvenile facility."

"On the streets, I think."

I see their faces in the team photos — the kids here and there who drifted away as the teenage years hit: troubled kids who would never say it aloud but were desperately seeking someone to believe in them.

At the time, did I step to the plate to be that someone?

I think of these kids like I think of the homeless: How did they get this way? Where do they sleep? Where do they go from here? Who watches out for them?

I realize help is a two-way street. Offering it isn't always enough; it must be accepted. And some boys I coached had hearts so hardened that it seemed nothing would penetrate that protective shield — not encouragement, not praise, not a challenge.

In such dilemmas, coaches find themselves like the father in Norman Maclean's *A River Runs Through It* who laments not being able to help his troubled youngest son. How do you reach someone, he ponders, who doesn't want to be reached?

I recall the boy whose father once dropped him off at a game and went to play tavern darts with a girlfriend — and missed his son's game-winning hit in the third extra inning.

I recall the boy who didn't even know who his father was and who never stayed in one place long enough to establish any sense of security.

And I recall the boy whose life was shattered one evening when his father left him alone, called the boy's uncle to come take care of the boy, then left to shoot himself.

I saw that little boy the other day. When he shuffled into the courtroom, hands and ankles shackled and with a sheriff's deputy at his side, I hardly recognized him. But, then, 16 years is a long time. He was now 26, not 10.

The deputy sat him in the juror's box. Last week, the jury sitting there had found him guilty on all nine counts stemming from a botched robbery attempt in Veneta involving two accomplices. Now it was time for sentencing.

On the night before the sentencing, I'd found the 1989-90 team photo: seven players and me mugging for the camera. One player is giving me rabbit ears. The boy is pulling on his ears and sticking out his lips, looking a little like Mr. Potato Head.

His powder blue uniform has a number "9." Now, in the courtroom, his deep green uniform reads "Lane Co. Jail."

He was planning on being married this summer. Now this. When I first heard the news, I thought of the kid whose father had killed himself. Mr. Potato Head. The young man now standing before a judge and reading a handwritten note.

"To all who suffered," he began, "I take full responsibility. I deeply apologize for my wrongful actions."

His voice quivered. "If I could go back to any one day and change it, Dec. 6 would be it. I don't expect anyone to forgive me, but this is all I have to offer. I'm deeply sorry."

When he finished speaking, the judge sentenced him to 192 months in prison.

As coaches, teachers and mentors, it's as if we work on assembly lines, charged with putting one tiny piece in lives that briefly glide by. We hope our contribution somehow makes them better. But we have no control over the larger pieces that have come before. Or those that will come after.

I no longer coach. Someday, though, I might return, perhaps pick up a group of ragamuffins who can't find a coach. If so, I need to remember the boy whose father killed himself, even if it isn't a pretty thought.

Need to to be there for the kid who's not getting any positive strokes from those around him.

Need to remember that, though the team photos always show smiling children in matching uniforms, such photos sometimes hide the lives beyond.

Like black ice beneath a snowy country road.

Hot box

I was pounding in bases, preparing for the first practice with the new seventh-grade team I would be coaching and feeling good for a couple of reasons:

First, it was May, meaning the base spikes would bore through the soggy Oregon soil with ease; by August, those same spikes would look like stainless steel curly fries, humbled by rock-hard dirt that had all the give of Hoover Dam.

Second, tryout week was over. I hate tryout week. In only three practices, you must select the best 15 baseball players out of about 50 kids. That's the easy part. The hard part is breaking the hearts of 35 players and about three times that many parents and stepparents and grandparents, some of whom think you're some sort of magic genie who can make their dreams come true. One year, a couple of boys were so upset at not being chosen that they bicycled by one of our practices with a paintball gun and nailed our leftfielder in the leg.

Ah, but that was all behind me now. The teams had been divided, the players had been notified, and it was time to start grooming this squad for the season ahead.

Suddenly, as I hammered the last peg at second base, a shadow appeared next to me. Turning, I realized it belonged to a man I knew — a man I knew whose son's dream hadn't come true. I had cut his kid.

"Well, you really blew it this time, Welch," said the man, his voice laced with venom.

The worst moment in journalism is when you're reading a story you've written and realize you've made an error. You've done someone irreparable harm. You think, momentarily, of all those tens of thousands of papers that are on people's doorsteps with your mistake in it, and you get this pit in your stomach, the "I-wish-I'd-been-a-milkman" feeling that hearkens back to those college days when you were going to bag the pressure of journalism for the simplicity of delivering milk, a job whose biggest screwup might mean someone eats their Frosted Flakes with skim instead of 2%.

That's how I felt when the man said I'd blown it: like I'd made some terrible mistake.

"How many years has my son made your team? Now this. This is just great. His brother gets cut from his team last night. Now this. Thanks a bunch."

I didn't say anything, just started walking toward first base to hammer down the final bag. My silence was partly because I didn't know what to say and partly because I'm the nonconfrontive sort. But I felt like I'd been kicked in the gut. This was a man who had been an assistant coach for me in years past, a guy who had kept our team's scorebook.

"I thought newspaper reporters were supposed to be objective," the man said. "Not in this case. You seemed a little biased toward your son's friends."

My heart was pounding. The guy wasn't letting up. Do I just let it go?

I let it go. I said nothing, just began pounding in the first-base bag.

"I hope you're proud of yourself," he huffed in conclusion. "I hope you can sleep tonight."

And off he stomped.

Maybe he was right; maybe I had blown it. Maybe I had been biased. Maybe I wouldn't sleep tonight.

But in the weeks to come, I confirmed within myself that I'd made the right decision; it was his problem, not mine. I told the story to friends of mine, who assured me I was right and the man was wrong. Still, the criticism stung.

I don't like relationships with untied knots; "If it is possible, as far as it depends on you, live at peace with everyone," says Romans 12:18.

Looking back, I can think of only a few people with whom I've had falling-outs that hadn't healed. But reconciliation didn't look likely with this rift.

Maybe I should call this guy and politely but firmly speak my mind. Tell him he'd wounded me. Explain why I'd made the choice I'd made. See if he might be willing to apologize so we could let it go.

But I didn't.

Occasionally, I'd see the man — he was helping coach his son's team — at the practice field. He avoided me. I avoided him. It was like that all summer long, two grown men seeing one another and pretending not to, each of us probably wondering what the other was thinking. It wore on me, week in and week out. And what bothered me more was that it probably wasn't wearing on him; otherwise, I figured, he would have called and apologized.

Maybe I should quit this silly coaching stuff, I thought. I'd been doing it for a decade. I didn't need this kind of friction; didn't need this guilt that I kept feeling, as if I were some ruthless king who had purposely denied a pauper's dream.

But I didn't. I finished the season, laughed at the team pizza party, dutifully turned in our team's equipment and returned to my post-baseball life. School started, followed by Oregon's famous winter rains, which seemed to wash away the memory of the confrontation.

That's all I needed, I realized: Time. Distance. Distractions. Stuff that would help me forget about something that had already cost me more mental hand-wringing than it deserved. Let him deal with it; it was his problem.

And that's exactly what happened: Work. Deadlines. Thanksgiving. Launching a book. Such stuff helped shove the incident far back in my mind's attic, back behind the Christmas tree ornaments and children's toys, so I could forget about it.

Until the morning of Christmas Eve. That's when our pastor gave a message that brought it all back, but in a new light. He spoke, naturally, about the birth of Christ. About God's Son come to Earth. About a humble peasant girl, great with child, who trusted that God was behind all this. About this Christ child being God's way of reconciling with man, His gift, given unconditionally for us, a bunch of sinners, including me.

So how, then, shall we live? the pastor asked. He flipped to 1 Peter 5:5. "All of you, clothe yourselves with humility toward one another, because God opposes the proud but gives grace to the humble."

Something stirred within me. We sang *O Little Town of Bethlehem* and something stirred even deeper, especially when I sang the lines:

> Yet in thy dark streets shineth
> The everlasting Light;
> The hopes and fears of all the years
> Are met in thee tonight

I've always loved those lines, but now they took on an added sense of urgency. That everlasting light was shining in my attic, illuminating my own hopes and fears. The time, I realized, had come.

When we arrived home from church, I searched the phone book, found the man's name, and started to make the call. He's probably not home, I reasoned, and cradled the receiver.

Make the call.

I picked up the phone. But what was I going to say? I had no idea. I held the phone in both hands, undecided.

Make the call.

But he'll think I'm nuts. He won't even remember the incident. I'll be totally embarrassed.

Make the call.

I punched the number and mumbled a silent prayer; God deserved better.

The man's wife answered.

"It's Bob Welch," I heard her whisper to her husband. In the seconds before he came on the phone, I wondered what the mention of my name would trigger in him. Anger? Bitterness? Or maybe nothing. Maybe he hadn't thought about the incident since it happened, and the joke was on me, because it had eaten away at me like an ulcer for the last six months.

That's OK, I figured, because what mattered now wasn't his attitude, but mine. I'd once been to a Promise Keepers event in which an African-American man — a man who had been wronged in ways that made any incivilities against me seem trivial by comparison — said something so profound I've never forgotten: At times someone will wrong you — and your pride will preclude you from trying to reconcile with that person. You may even be clearly right and the other person clearly wrong.

"The question is this," he said: "Would you rather be right, or would you rather be reconciled?"

In a sense, we occasionally find ourselves in a relational hot box, a rundown between pride and humility. And pride is the base we naturally head for.

... Or would you rather be reconciled?

The seconds it took for the man to pick up the phone seemed like hours. But eventually he came on the line. Every now and then, God moves people to do things they could never do without Him, like those people you read about in *Reader's Digest* who summon the strength to lift a minivan that's crushing some little boy and then later have no idea how they did it.

That's what God did in this instance. What I told the man was nothing eloquent. It was stilted. It was jittery and jagged and came out of left field — a grown man telling another grown man, a guy he hardly knew, that he was sorry. That he'd just been to church and felt convicted to call and make things right. And that he'd made mistakes before in choosing teams, and probably would next year, too, and, well, he hoped the man would forgive him for not choosing his son last summer.

The man on the other end of the line dropped his guard. He told of how hurt his older son had been in not making the team he'd hoped to make; when the same thing happened to his younger son the next day, the man had snapped. He was sorry for his actions, too. Sorry he'd unloaded on me as he had.

They were both sorry. It was Christmas Eve.

"Merry Christmas," I said.

"And Merry Christmas to you," he said.

Before the next season began, I'd already decided it would be my last year of coaching. My youngest son, whose team I had coached for five years, would be in the high school program and others would coach him. The time had come to hang up the whistle — or at least take a long sabbatical.

But our last year together was a great year. We had a mediocre team but we played hard and pulled some big upsets. We beat one of those cocky teams with a coach who respects nobody, not even his own players. We won the consolation bracket championship. And we simply had fun, in part because of an assistant coach I'd invited to help me — the father of the boy I'd cut the previous year.

At times, during the season, I'd look over from my third-base box and see the man coaching first base, laughing, and giving base-running advice to my son, his son, and other people's sons — and I'd be reminded of one simple truth: the love of God can bore through hearts more resistant than a rock-hard infield in August.

Frog

He was the new kid at Garfield School, a sixth-grader who had just moved from Idaho. Given that state's abundance of a certain type of vegetable and our group's sense of humor and provinciality, we toyed with the idea of calling him "Mr. Potato Head." Based on his thick, black glasses, however, we settled instead on simply "Frog." I don't recall him doing anything in particular to offend us. Nor do I recall us blatantly bullying him.

I just recall subtly reminding him early on that we were here first and, thus, better than him.

Until, that is, he came out for flag football practice and we realized the kid had a cannon for an arm, was lightning fast and knew football like Hershey's knows chocolate. He certainly didn't look the part — he looked, well, kind of nerdy in those glasses. But anyone who could help us win football games was good enough for us; we offered him membership in our exclusive club.

I thought of "Frog" in the wake of the shootings at Columbine High School in Colorado. I thought of how easily we label people without even knowing them, particularly if we're insiders and, like "Frog," they're outsiders. I thought of how quick we are — even as adults — to decide who belongs in the inner circle and who does not.

Finally, I thought of how the Columbine killers specifically singled out jocks as targets. Their thinking? You've bullied us, ridiculed us, humiliated us. But, surprise, we bat last. They then stepped to the plate and began swinging unmercifully.

Nothing — absolutely nothing — justifies the bloody rampage that ensued. Nothing excuses murder. Nothing rationalizes the fact that 15 people are dead and the lives of those who knew them and loved them will never be the same. But amid such tragedy, we're negligent if, instead of pointing fingers at others, we don't also look in the mirror and try to learn something.

I realize it's a long way from a minor snub at Garfield School in the '60s to gunfire at Columbine High in the '90s, and yet the incidents touch on sports and exclusivity — who belongs and who does not.

As much as sports can bring together communities and individuals, they can also build walls between the perceived "haves" and "have-nots." At Columbine, the state wrestling champ was regularly permitted to park his $100,000 Hummer all day in a 15-minute space, the homecoming king was on probation for burglary and a football player was allowed to tease a girl in class without fear of retribution by his teacher, also the boy's coach.

As much as sports can produce the kind of heroes we desperately need, many athletes and coaches in America are accorded a place of honor that they don't deserve — pampered and indulged not because of any particular character quality, but because they can hit a curve ball or throw a tight spiral or coach a basketball team to a conference title.

As much as sports can teach lessons such as honesty, commitment and teamwork, so can they teach lessons of arrogance, selfishness, and bigotry.

When I was in high school, a bunch of jocks and one journalist/ jock (me) were riding in a car one winter evening, firing icy snowballs at oncoming cars. When one smacked like a rock into the windshield of a car, I said enough. We needed to stop; someone was going to get hurt. My friends just laughed, so I got out of the car and walked a mile home in the dark.

Years later, the incident would remind me that power turns ugliest when it's the result of majority-rules thinking based solely on concern for one's self. It leads to countries starting wars. It leads to high school cliques bullying those who don't belong. It leads to racism and sexism. And sometimes, it leads to the kind of self-righteous thinking that angered Jesus like nothing else.

He hated the idea of people lording power over others. Wrote the Apostle Paul:

> Do nothing out of selfish ambition or vain conceit, but in humility consider others better than yourselves. Each of you should look not only to your own interests, but also to the interests of others.
>
> Your attitude should be the same as Christ Jesus: Who, being in very nature God, did not consider equality with God something to be grasped, but made himself nothing, taking the very nature of a servant."
> (Philippians 2:3-7)

The verses suggest honor and integrity have nothing to do with the group to which we belong and everything to do with our hearts. Translating that thinking to Garfield School, 1965, my pals and I would have accepted "Frog" whether or not he wore thick, black glasses, and whether or not he could throw a football. Instead, in a sense, he had to prove himself worthy of our standards.

A few years ago, I was asked to return to my old high school and speak to the newspaper class. A classmate of mine was on hand, too. We were two very different people — in high school, she had been part of what was called the "Folk Dancers" clique, more apt to be spending a Friday night reading poetry or smoking pot than attend a football game. When our presentations to the newspaper class were finished, we talked briefly about our high school days and how rigid had been the boundaries between groups.

"If I had to do it over again, I think it would have been fun to be in a play," I told her.

"Hey, I confess," she said, "I looked at everyone involved in Spirit Week and thought: That looks like fun."

But of course, The Rules wouldn't allow us such access to enemy camps — as if we were all dogs penned in by those invisible fences.

Our conversation was encouraging because it reminded me that people can change and grow and gain perspective. Looking back on my school days, I realize how painfully easy it was to pigeon-hole people as this or that without even knowing who they were. And how small-minded we were in according respect only to those who had proven to us, in our Pharisee-like arrogance, that they could further our cause.

I think of one young man named Mike Riley, who graduated from high school a year ahead of me. He was a jock, but not one of those who lorded that identity above anyone else. He was tremendously talented but equally humble and shy, a guy who helped lead our school to state titles in three sports, yet remained this unassuming presence whose heart always seemed to be in the right place.

After high school, Riley played college football under the legendary Bear Bryant at Alabama and became a coach. In Canada, his Winnipeg teams won two Grey Cup titles, that country's equivalent of our Super Bowl, then coached in the United State Football League and at Southern California.

He's now head coach at Oregon State — and walks the sidelines of a stadium where we used to hop the fence and play in back in the '60s.

When I think of Mike Riley, I'm reminded that not all nice guys finish last. I'm also reminded that some people who like to think they're nice guys — people like me — need to remember that we all have a little Pharisee blood in us and need to be careful about exalting ourselves while putting down those around us until they earn the keys to our clique.

Back at Garfield School, you see, we had a nickname for Mike Riley.

It was "Frog."

Glory and grace

In October 1998, Linfield College in McMinnville, Oregon, — a college with fewer students than some high schools — broke a national football record that had stood for 66 years and had been held by two of the country's most esteemed institutions: Notre Dame and Harvard. It clinched the school's 43rd consecutive winning season — a longer streak than any of the nearly 700 schools on any collegiate level had ever established.

Each year since 1956, Linfield has had more wins in a season than losses. The streak, still going strong through the 2005 season even though the Wildcats have stepped up from the NAIA level to NCAA Division III level, has spanned 10 U.S. presidents, four wars and parts of six decades. It began before NASA was founded, before desktop computers and artificial turf were invented and before some of the parents of the current team were born.

Following the 2005 season, the streak stood at an even 50.

To put the accomplishment in perspective, realize that Harvard's 42-year streak began in 1881, only two decades after the start of the Civil War, and stretched to 1923; Notre Dame's ran from 1889 to three years after the stock market crash of '29. So you can understand why the Linfield students felt compelled to rip down the goal posts when the record was broken.

Selfishly, I would like to believe the record was established because the coach at the time, Jay Locey, is a close friend of mine and was the best man at my wedding. I would like to believe it was established because I so inspired Locey with my athletic prowess when we played Little League baseball together — he was on the Owls and I on the Loons — or because I taught him the "Gambler's Bet" offense in a dice football game or because I dragged him on high-lake backpacking trips that taught him tenacity (not to mention "never spit with mosquito netting over your face") when we were in college.

But I really think the school's success — Linfield won the NCAA Division III championship in 2004 — rests on the strength of a legacy. Oh sure, it had something to do with X's and O's, a fumbled ball that bounced right when it could have bounced left, a blue-chip recruit here and there. But more than anything, I believe the all-time record was established by Linfield because of the four coaches who started and continued that legacy.

Each of them had his own style; clones they were not. But each carried themselves as if the school, the program, the legacy were more important than themselves. Above all, they instilled two important principles in their players: First, that the players were expected to win. And, second, that they were valued highly even if they didn't. In other words, their worth was not solely dependent on what they accomplished on the field.

Some young people are being brought up by parents who place high expectations on their children, but whose love for their children is conditional. Such parents leave legacies in those kids of high achievement and low self-esteem. Their children accomplish much but never enough to satisfy the parents.

Other young people are being brought up by parents who love their children, win or lose, but expect so little from them that their kids have no inspiration to become all they were meant to be. Such parents leave legacies in their children of unrealized growth.

Once, while driving across Oregon's Coast Range, I saw a tree so ablaze with autumn that it looked like a multicolored Popsicle. It was so vibrant that, at first glance, I didn't think it was real. Looking back, I realize that it may never have been more real. This was the deepest expression of its being, the height of its glory, nature bringing forth its best.

I believe God designed us to be so fully involved living the "abundant life" that, at times, we should look like that tree. But He doesn't abandon us when we don't. Though He wants us to be vibrant, He loves us no less when we're leafless limbs on a winter's day. He forgives us for not being perfect. In short, He grants us grace.

In his book *What's So Amazing About Grace*, author Philip Yancey says that of all the religions, only Christianity "dares to make God's love unconditional." We cannot work hard enough to earn his favor; we cannot fail badly enough to lose it.

Without putting Locey and the other coaches on some divine pedestal, I believe what they've done with their players is similar: expected much and forgiven much. That's not customary in sports. In the NFL, much is expected and little forgiven; it's not uncommon for the guy who misses the would-be game-winning field goal on Sunday to be released from the team on Monday. And, sadly, youth sports programs are sprinkled with coaches who coach with the same cutthroat philosophy. I still can't forget a TV investigative report in which a coach, knowing full well he was on camera, angrily chastising a player for striking out, then warns that there would be a price to pay later.

It was the man's son.

That kind of attitude doesn't wash at Linfield. This is not a machine; as Ad Rutschman, who kept the streak alive as coach from 1968 to 1991, says: "I see our program as one giant classroom." Coaches don't see themselves as gods; in fact, humility has been a trademark of all four men, the first in this four-man relay being Paul Durham, and Ed Langsdorf sandwiched between Rutschman and Locey, who left Linfield in the summer of 2006 to coach at Oregon State, his alma mater.

"In theory, all college coaches talk about teaching values," said Mike Riley, a former Linfield assistant and now head coach at Oregon State. "But at Linfield it's actually done."

And also at Oregon State, Riley would prove in years to come. On the first Saturday of the college football season in 2004, Riley's Beavers — heavy underdogs — outplayed defending co-national champion Louisiana State all night long. But Alexis Serna, a walk-on redshirt freshman placekicker, had a horrid night. He missed all three of his PAT attempts and LSU won 22-21 in overtime.

"I didn't feel safe," the 5-foot-7 Serna said about being in the Oregon State locker room after the game. "Guys were yelling at me. Other people were holding them back. I didn't know what they were going to do."

Serna lay sprawled out on the locker room floor, crying. "Finally one of the coaches told me to pick myself up and take a shower." He didn't know that ESPN had an overhead camera in the visitors' locker room and that the entire country could watch his meltdown.

In Corvallis, at a Beaver friend's house, I was among them. "There's a kid," I said, "who'll never play another down of college football."

Riley believed otherwise. He sat Serna one game, then gave him another chance. Serna converted 24 of 24 PAT attempts and 16 of 17 field goal attempts, including a 55-yarder at Washington. In late November, Riley awarded him a scholarship.

The next year Serna led the nation in points. He scored all 18 of OSU's points in an 18-10 win over Washington in the rain. And won the Lou Groza Award as the top placekicker in the nation, making 62 straight extra-points since the LSU game the previous year.

In part, because Riley — in the tradition he'd been grounded in at Linfield — expected much. And forgave much.

Would that we, as parents, could leave such a legacy with our children: the realization that they are part of something ongoing, something significant that existed long before they arrived and will exist long after they've left, but right now, is depending on them to carry on.

I've read about young gang members who defend their life of violence and self-destruction by saying, "Why not? I don't have any-thing to lose." They feel so detached from anything or anybody that life becomes cheap. To lose, then, is to lose nothing; to take someone else's life, then, is to take nothing. But a Linfield player takes the field knowing there's much to lose: pride, a game, the continuation of a legacy. And when there's something to lose, there's motivation to win.

When Linfield has fallen behind, both in games and in seasons, the team has an incredible record for rallying. What that suggests is play-ers who have more than speed, strength and finesse; in addition, it's players who have character, perseverance and the will to overcome; players and coaches who, when their backs are to the wall, keep cool and trust each other instead of panicking and blaming each other.

In 1987, Linfield began the season 1-4 and had lost games by 24, 21 and 18 points; one more loss in the next four games and the winning-record streak — at the time, 33 years — would be over.

One rainy practice, Rutschman, brooding along the sidelines in his rain suit and rubber boots, couldn't watch another dropped pass or botched hand-off. He slammed down his clipboard (even nice guys get peeved occasionally) and ordered the team to the locker room.

"He never once called us losers or said he was ashamed of us," said offensive guard Joe Brims. "He just told us that we weren't being all we should be. That's the thing with Rutschman: He just wanted us to get the most out of ourselves."

He expected more from them because he knew they had more to give. And he got it. Linfield proceeded to win its next three games by an average of 20 points to go 4-4, then rallied in the second half of its final game to clinch yet another winning season.

In 1990, a former Linfield player, Jim Winston, found himself facing long odds himself. He had been paralyzed in a car accident. As he lay in a Los Angeles hospital, what he found himself thinking back to was the undefeated national championship Linfield team he had played on.

He remembered how the coach, on the eve of a game, would say something like, "Tomorrow, gentlemen, you will face adversity every single play. How you react to that adversity will determine who wins. And it will be that way tomorrow, five years from now – every single day of your life."

Within days of Winston's accident, Rutschman got on the phone to his former defensive tackle, encouraging him not to quit. "I've never forgotten how he told the team that self-pity leads to self destruction," said Winston.

Since then, Winston has gotten married, works in the television industry and still feels part of the Linfield legacy. "Here I am, paralyzed, and yet I still feel like I did when I was strong and fast and playing for Rutschman. I still feel like a winner."

Teams with character reach deep when they must; so do people whose battles are waged well beyond the chalked lines of a football field — people who are encouraged to soar but are loved even when they don't.

— From *Where Roots Grow Deep.*

Final season

The other night, after the parents had all come to pick up their sons and I was picking up catchers' equipment, bats and, of course, one forgotten mitt, it dawned on me that this was it: the last season I would coach one of my sons' baseball teams. Twelve seasons. Two sons. Hundreds of games. Maybe three decent umps. And thousands of memories, hidden in my mind like all those foul balls lost in the creek behind the Ascot Park backstop.

Sitting in the bleachers on this spring evening — everyone had gone — I found myself lost in thought. Found myself mentally walking along the creek, finding those long-forgotten baseballs and listening to the stories each had to tell.

The time our left field got locked in a Dairy Queen bathroom during a post-game celebration ... The time I handed a protective cup to our new catcher and he thought it was an oxygen mask ... The time a tee-baller cleanly fielded a grounder, picked it up and tossed it to his mom, who was sitting on the third-base sidelines, reading Gone With the Wind.

For something that became more than a decade-long family affair, it had begun casually enough. While I was watching one of my 5-year-old son's tee-ball games in 1985, a manager asked if I would coach second base.

"Uh, *second* base?"

"Yeah. At this level you need coaches at second or the kids will forget to take a left and wind up at Safeway."

So I coached second base. And before long, our family's summers revolved around a diamond: me coaching, my wife, Sally, keeping score and the boys playing. Like the Israelites trudging out of Egypt, we packed our equipment, lawn chairs, video camera and 64-ounce drinks from diamond to diamond, week after week, summer after summer.

> *The time our right fielder turned up missing during a championship game, only to be found at the snack bar eating licorice and flirting with girls ... The time we showed up at an empty field, only to discover I had read the schedule wrong and our game was actually 10 miles away ... The time I explained to my fifth-grade team that, because we had given up 89 runs in the last four games, we needed to set a defensive goal.*

"It's a six-inning game," I said. "Let's see if we can hold them to 12 runs per game. Two per inning. Can you do that?"

Silence. Then my philosophical right fielder spoke up.

"Coach," he said, "do we have to give up the runs even like that or could we, like, give up all 12 in one inning?"

Our teams were more than a collection of kids. They were extended family, some of whom wound up sleeping overnight. And some of the boys desperately needed that. One year, of 15 players, only five had a mother and father living together under the same roof. Once, a boy missed practice because his uncle had been murdered. And sometimes I took kids home because nobody came to pick them up.

> *The out-of-control coach who pushed me off the field ... The kid who didn't get picked for my team and sought revenge by firing a paint gun at our left fielder during a practice ... And the father who dropped off his son, Willie, and told him to get his own ride home; he and his girlfriend were going to a tavern to play darts. We went into three extra innings that afternoon and the man's son played the game of his life, going all nine innings at catcher. As dusk tinted the game with added drama, he ripped the game-winning hit.*

We tried to make it more than just baseball. With help from our sons, we established a team newspaper. A few times, I would put candy in a sack at second base and let players dig in every time they made an out. (Best defensive practice we ever had.) My wife Sally played DH — designated healer — with her ever-present cooler full of pop, and packages of frozen corn for the sprained ankles and bruised arms. Once we had pizza delivered to the ball field just after we had lost to the same team with the coach who pushed me off the field. I think we had more fun that night than the team that won.

> *A weak-hitting kid named Cody stroking a three-run double and later telling his mom: "I try to stop smiling, but I just can't." … My older son, Ryan, becoming an assistant coach and reaching a few kids in ways that I could not … A rainy April evening, my entire team crammed into my parked Subaru station wagon as I stood outside under an umbrella, quizzing them on defensive situations.*

And, of course, the night we were going to win the city championship. Our team that year was a team of destiny. We won games we had no business winning. In the quarterfinals, we needed three runs in the bottom of the last inning with the weakest part of the order at bat. We won. I could taste our first-ever city championship.

But the game never got played. After a rainless summer, the skies opened up on the night of the championship game. The two teams were declared co-champs. I couldn't believe the officials wouldn't allow us to play the game at a later date. *There's no tying in baseball.*

Until now apparently. We had a sort-of-celebration at a pizza parlor. After everyone had left, the restaurant manager approached me, broom in hand. "Excuse me, but are you the coach of the Washington Braves?"

"I sure am," I said, suddenly feeling a flicker of pride on the brink of this compliment.

He handed me the broom. "Your team trashed the indoor playroom. There's broken peppermint candy everywhere. Wanna help sweep?"

Somehow, this is not how I thought I would end this day of destiny: sweeping up a pizza parlor playroom, all alone, on a rainy night.

Regrets? Sitting in the bleachers, looking back, I could think of only one. Sure, I would have loved that championship. But more than that, I wish Willie's father had considered his son more important than a game of darts and had stayed to see him mobbed by teammates after making that game-winning hit. Everyone saw it but the guy who needed to see it most.

My life's work is not work. Indiana basketball coach Bobby Knight likes to say of sportswriters, "We all learn to write by second grade; most of move on to bigger things." Most of us stop throwing chairs and calling ourselves Bobby by the second grade, too. But I see his point.

— Steve Rushin in *Road Swing: One Fan's Journey into the Soul of American Sports*

4

The
Sportswriter

On his 5th birthday, left, the author got an electric football set,
admired here by his uncle, Bob
Schumacher. Years later, after
playing a game with the plastic
players, inset, he would write a short story, complete with statistics, and draw a "photograph"
of the game. The drawing, above, was done
when he was 7. Note the enormous football and
the facemasks on the players, which his mother
mistook for large noses.

Electric football

If I mention it during a speech, invariably a handful of baby-boom-aged men will head toward me afterward like bugs to a No-Pest Strip. They want me to know that they had one, too. They loved it, too. And they haven't forgotten theirs, either: the Tudor Tru-Action Electric Football game.

If there was a quintessential game for baby boom boys during the '60s, this was it.

The game was a cookie sheet-like field about the size of a door-mat. On it, 22 two-inch, plastic men, red and yellow, jiggled around as if the team manager had put Deep Heat in their jockstraps.

To play, you lined up an offense and a defense, stuffed a felt "football" in the arm of the ball carrier, clicked a power switch and — voila! — nobody went where they were expected to. The game ran on vibrations, not always good. Indeed, each "play" took about five minutes to set up and less than five seconds to self-destruct. Your left end, his nylon runners bent, might be doing circles like a merry-go-round. Your right guard might be bumping incessantly against the opposition's sidelines.

You would plan for your tailback to, say, run off right tackle; instead, he would bump into his left guard, turn around and run 80 yards the wrong way.

For passes, you brought in "Springman," half human being, half metal catapult. You loaded the felt ball into his spring-loaded "bucket," cocked it, pinched the "action clasp" and — voila! — Springman would throw a pass out of the stadium and into your bedroom closet, soon to be scarfed up my your cocker spaniel, Jet.

Any successful play in Tudor Tru-Action Electric Football was a complete accident.

But it was awesome. After getting the game for my birthday when I was 5 — I used to think it was for Christmas when I was 11 but later found a photograph of me with it the night I received it — I would come home from school, line up the players and play. Bzzzzzzzzzzzzzz. "That thing sounded like a high-speed drill," my mother once told me.

Set up a play. Bzzzzzzzzzzzzzz. Set up a play. Bzzzzzzzzzzzzzz. And another … .

Then it happened: The unthinkable. I raced home from school one day, flipped the switch and — click — nothing happened. The game had broken. My life was suddenly empty.

But later, I got an idea: I took one player in my right hand and raced him down the sidelines, tackling him with a handful of players in my left. That's it! I could create my own games.

This way, runners could actually run toward the right goal. Springman could actually complete a pass. And, best of all, Oregon State— I grew up in Corvallis, home of the Beavers — could always win. In the six years between 1959 and 1965, the Beavers won a record 439 Rose Bowls.

In my best nasally voice, I became East Coast TV annoncer Lindsey Nelson. "Welcome to Parker Stadium," he would say, "home of the Ar-Uh-Gun State Beavers."

I stacked *World Book Encyclopedias* around the field as grandstands. ("Section Q? Yes, right, here ma'm, between 'P' and 'R.' ") I placed a desk lamp atop the books and turned off the bedroom lights to play night games. With model paint, I turned the sickly yellow players into orange-and-black Beavers.

My parents — secretly thrilled, I think, that the high-speed drill was doomed — even helped out. Dad made me goal posts out of coat hangers, complete with electrical-tape padding at the base. Mom donated a 78 rpm record of college fight songs she'd won at a bridge-club party; I played it before every game.

Ah, but I wasn't finished. I grabbed handfuls of mud from Mom's garden — remember, artificial turf wasn't used until the late '60s — to add to the authenticity. And then came the *coup de grace*: snow.

Ivory Soap flakes, of course. The snow looked awesome, but players hated it. Turns out I was allergic to the flakes and, with a single sneeze, could blow players off the field. (This led to the formation of a players' union, which demanded sneeze-freeze clauses in players' contracts.)

The fun didn't end when a game was over. Instead, at that point, I put on my sportswriter's hat. Using a Smith-Corona typewriter my mother had given me, I would write a short story, say, two or three sentences, compile some statistics and draw a crayon "photograph," complete with a caption. At age 7 — on Nov. 8, 1961 — I wrote:

> Stanford completed a pass on third down. in the first quarter. The defender was Don Kasso on Oregon State. He ticked the ball and then number 44 completed it on Stanford.

My sentences, often incomplete and eschewing capital letters, were a bit like e.e. cummings in a press box. And my "photographs" were hilarious: the football, in relation to the players, was usually the size of the Hindenburg. Beyond that, every picture would have a peculiarity that only recently my mother understood. "I could never understand why you gave the players such big noses," she said.

"Mom," I said. "Those weren't noses. Those were facemasks."

"Oh."

At the time, nobody knew that with each drawing, with each story, with each keystroke, I was doing essentially the same thing my grandfather, Will Adams, had done after playing sandlot baseball games in 1905. (See "Sandlot Journal," Page 204.) And nobody knew that I was preparing to be what I've been now for more than 30 years: a journalist.

For five or six years, I played Tudor Tru-Action Electric Football with no electricity, even as the number of players dwindled from 22 to nine to six, thanks to Jet, whose appetite, it turned out, went beyond errant cotton-ball passes. And thanks to my mother's vacuum cleaner, which had a similar appetite. Who knows how many players wound up in Mom's Hoover Hall of Fame.

But those who survived cleaning day and Jet were a gutsy bunch.

Talk about playing hurt. Some were missing body parts. Old-timers like to brag about the days of real football, when guys played without helmets. That's nothing. I had guys who played without *heads* — and made All-American.

Finally, my mother intervened. "I think it's time for you to give up the game," she said.

"But *Mom*," I protested.

"Bob, there are other things in life."

"But Mom!" I protested.

"Bob, you're leaving for college tomorrow."

And so I grew up. But I never forgot the Tudor Tru-Action football set. And, actually, neither did my mother. She saved it for me. Nearly half a century after I first played the game, it hangs in our house basement stairwell: a rusted, bent, semi-green piece of metal. It looks pathetic, really, like something you wouldn't want hanging in your house. I take it to elementary schools when I talk to kids about writing and, invariably, they're fascinated by it.

It reminds the students, as it reminds me, that anything is possible when you discover that a game — or life for that matter — doesn't need electricity in order to run. It can run on something far more powerful:

Imagination. The ability to see not what *is,* but what *might be*.

Dream makers

A rocket won't fly unless somebody lights the fuse.
— Homer Hickam Jr., *October Sky*

In 1965, my fifth-grade teacher at Garfield Elementary School in Corvallis, Oregon, stood in front of the class and boldly announced that Career Day was coming. Her name was Mrs. Wirth. She had red hair, perfect cursive writing and that sort of youthful enthusiasm that would later remind me of TV's *Mary Tyler Moore.*

Her eyes scanned the room as if searching for life's possibilities. "So, people," she said, "what do you want to be when you grow up?"

She then told us that each of us would get to choose someone from the community who does a job related to our field of interest. She would try to arrange for us to watch that person in action and to ask them questions.

We had a week to decide who that person might be, but I already knew. When it was time to make our choice, Mrs. Wirth went alphabetically through the class until she came to the "W's."

"And, Mr. Welch, what would you like to do?" she asked.

At age 11, I was a freckle-faced wonder with a crew cut and

enough butch wax on my forehead to mortar The Great Wall of China. I didn't know much about a lot of things, including why everyone in the world but me had a Sting-Ray bike. But I did know what I wanted to be when I grew up.

"I want to interview Paul Valenti, the Oregon State basketball coach," I said. "I want to be a sportswriter."

Mrs. Wirth looked at me and nodded one of those nods that began as surprise and evolved into affirmation.

She was a fresh-from-college school teacher, not some veteran miracle worker. And she held in her hands the futures of 29 kids, one of whom had just boldly asked for the moon.

Paul Valenti, meanwhile, was a major-college basketball coach in his first year of trying to replace the legendary Slats Gill. Gill had been the head coach at OSU since 1929, the year the stock market crashed. He had won 599 games and nine conference titles and was so revered in Corvallis that they named the basketball arena after him after he retired. The pressure on Valenti was considerable.

But when a young school teacher called to see if Valenti would give half an hour to an 11-year-old boy, he said yes. The rest, as they say, is history, recorded on the pages of The Garfield Chatter, a school newspaper that published the story written by me and two buddies who helped me interview the coach.

Dreams, I've come to believe, are almost always partnerships. They require a dreamer and a dream maker; someone with the vision to go someplace and someone willing to help the person get there.

Mrs. Wirth could easily have said my request was out of reach; couldn't I choose something a bit less ambitious? But instead she made it happen. So she's among those I've always credited for helping me become a writer.

Others helped. So did journalistic genes. In 1905, my grandfather, Will Adams, not only kept an illustrated and box-scored baseball journal that ultimately wound up being given to me, but he and his pals published something called The Hooligan Gazette. It was a neighborhood newspaper in which sports stories were sprinkled amid features on bicycle-propelled airships and — clearly ahead of his times — alien-abductions.

My father was a photographer and an artist, a man whose creativity showed through in pictures and drawings, in movies and Christmas cards and sketches of sailboats on the water.

At 7, my scrapbook will attest, I was already creating newspaper sports pages, almost exclusively about Oregon State University football. At 9, I had already photographed a Corvallis-Sweet Home basketball game. And at 12, I received the kind of Christmas present few 12-year-olds receive from their parents: a subscription to *Sports Illustrated*; the next year, I got a desk on which to place my Smith-Corona typewriter.

When our local newspaper, the *Corvallis Gazette-Times*, needed a representative from my junior high basketball team to phone in game results, I eagerly volunteered. The morning after each game, I would call Jack Rickard, the sports editor, and read him the final score, points for each player, and the score by quarters. After saying each name, I could hear the staccato click of his typewriter as he translated my words to paper. It was miraculous.

After getting home from basketball practice that night, there it would be: a story in the *Gazette-Times* about our team's latest loss, complete with the names and numbers I'd phoned in just that morning. Amazing!

If this job got my foot in the door, Little League baseball swung it wide open. Would I be interested, asked Mr. Rickard, in compiling the town's baseball results for a story each day during the summer?

It was like Wendy being asked by Peter Pan if she wanted to fly. Each evening, a Parks and Recreation guy would deliver to my house the results from dozens and dozens of games. I typed those results into one long story. And because there were so many games and because I didn't want my copy to grow stale, I created a systematic approach.

I created a list of every verb I could think of that described what one team could do to another:

trim
edge
down
nip
clip
whip
trip
top
stop
drop
bounce

blank
thrash
trash
thump
crush
cream
cruise past
slip by
roll over
turn back
outslug
outlast ...

and, my personal favorite — a word that I always thought gave me such a sense of sophistication because of its length and challenging spelling — "annihilate."

Nobody in my stories ever hit a triple; they "lashed" a triple. Nobody ever pitched a two-hitter; they "twirled" a two-hitter. I wrote of 31-0 games, of Steve Schmidt's unassisted triple play, of the Flying Saucers whipping the Astros and the Moonblasters thrashing the Fireballs.

My first byline appeared as "Tom Welch," the kind of mistake in which the half-right factor offers little in the way of consolation. But how could I complain? I was being paid $35 a summer for something I loved to do, a hefty sum for which I felt slightly guilty.

My love for sportswriting deepened. I began reading all the greats from the past, including Grantland Rice and Red Smith. Writing about four key Notre Dame players in a 1924 football game, Rice once began one of the most notable sports stories in history like this: "Outlined against a blue-gray October sky, the Four Horsemen rode again ... ."

I never wrote anything quite that artsy in the Little League round-ups — usually, it was something more like "Tom Boubel lashed two triples as the Cobras creamed the Cheetahs 12-2 Thursday ..." — but I dreamed I someday would.

I became sports editor of my junior high newspaper and then my high school newspaper, both of which were advised by a man, Jim Macpherson, who was like my Mr. Holland of journalism. We called him "Mac." He inspired us to reach for the stars — and the dictionary. What's more, when a typewriter fell out of the newspaper's third-floor office — we'd been using it to prop open a window because we were getting hot playing an impromptu baseball game in celebration of making deadline — he forgave us.

When the *Gazette-Times'* Rickard asked if I wanted to cover some high school football games, I told my folks I was going to actually be sitting in a press box, a place of such utter privilege that I scarcely believed my good fortune. A few days later, they surprised me with a new pair of binoculars.

In the summers, I started reading the masters: Ernest Hemingway and William Faulkner, John Steinbeck and Flannery O'Connor. I dutifully clipped out the monthly "Word Power" features in *Reader's Digest* and, during breaks at work on a spot-fire crew, had a co-worker test me on them. Once, on a weekend backpacking trip, I skimmed through an entire dictionary, a feat which friends still chide me about more than 30 years later.

Meanwhile, I went from being sports editor of my high school newspaper in Corvallis to sports editor of my college newspaper 40 miles away in Eugene, having the misfortune of serving at a time when the University of Oregon's 14-game football losing streak was the longest in the nation. By the time the Ducks finally snapped their 392-day victory drought, so few people were in the stands that, from the press box, we joked that instead of introducing the players to the fans, it would be faster to introduce the fans to the players.

Throughout college, I worked part-time in the sports department at *The Register-Guard*, the local daily. On Friday nights, the pattern was six hours of game-watching, car-driving, deadline-hovering, story-writing, phone-answering chaos. Once, a copy editor named Paul Harvey, a gruff guy who smoked like a chimney and loved model trains, kept looking at his watch and pestering me to finish my story.

"Not quite finished," I said, tapping away on the Royal.

"You are now," he said, and literally ripped the story out of the typewriter, slapped a headline on it, and sent it downstairs to be typeset.

After my shift ended and my adrenaline ebbed, I would take the elevator to the basement, buy a 50-cent hot dog from the vending machine, put it in the microwave, and think the same thought each week: *Could life get any better than this?*

I graduated from college and became sports editor of a small daily newspaper in Central Oregon. A few years later, Bob Chandler, the publisher of the paper, took me to lunch at a place called Tony's Poco

Toro, the only restaurant I've ever eaten in that had red crushed lava rock on its roof. Mr. Chandler, about 60 at the time, looked a little like actor Lionel Barrymore. From his shirt pocket he pulled out a small substance of what looked like a chocolate brownie wrapped in cellophane, took a plug, and extended it to me. It was chewing tobacco.

"Care for some?"

"Uh, no thanks."

He then wrapped it back up, stuck it in his pocket, and said, "So, Welch, what do you want to be when you grow up?"

I laughed lightly. I was, of course, quite sure of the fact that I was quite grown up. I was happy being a sportswriter.

He listened, or pretended to, then said, "Welch, you're one of the first sports editors we've ever had who actually had an English class before he got here. You can't spell worth beans, but other than that, you know the language. But you can't cover Bend High football games the rest of your life."

I took that as a compliment from a man who issued them with roughly the frequency of the Olympic Games — every four years. But still, how can you aspire to be more when you don't see any "more" to reach?

"This is all I've ever wanted to be," I said.

He paused, then said something I'll never forget.

"Be more," he said.

People joke about sportswriters working in the "toy department," but anyone who's watched what they do behind the scenes — say, write a game story in 45 minutes at 11 p.m. — know how hard they work. His point wasn't that there was something unworthy about being a sportswriter, only that there was nowhere else for me to go in sports in this town. And I needed to keep challenging myself.

So he offered me a job as editor of paper's new Sunday edition.

Looking back, I later realized he was right. In the years to come, I would leave sports, become a features writer, then a columnist. I would start writing for magazines, then write books. And I would wind up one day at Oregon State University, giving a reading from *A Father for All Seasons,* a book about fathers and sons that I'd written after my father died in 1996.

It was, in a sense, a homecoming. This was Corvallis, my old hometown, a few hundred yards from where it all began, where I'd interviewed Paul Valenti 33 years before for the *Garfield Chatter.*

I was reading a chapter when, looking up from the book, my eyes scanned the room. That's when I saw her in the audience: a red-headed woman who looked to be in her 50s. For an instant, I hesitated, smiled ever so slightly, then continued on with my story.

As I glanced at her from time to time, her eyes said the same thing they'd said to me back in that fifth-grade classroom in 1965. Said the same thing that the other dream makers had said to me all along, whether it was through a gift of binoculars, a lesson on writing or the simple encouragement to be more.

What that look said is: I believe in you.

Still.

Press box

During my first week as an official newspaper reporter, I called the local high school football coach and asked if I could come interview him the next day. He said fine.

As I drove to his house, I remember thinking that I had finally arrived. I was no longer writing Little League baseball stories with misspelled bylines. I was no longer working for the student daily between lit and poly-sci classes. I was no longer a part-timer at *The Register-Guard,* writing stories that would get ripped out of my typewriter by impatient editors.

Instead, at age 22, I was a player in the game of life — the sports editor of a small but thriving metropolis newspaper, *The Bulletin* in Bend, Oregon. (OK, a town of about 17,000 at the time, but compared with the blink-and-miss towns of Central and Eastern Oregon, a relative metropolis.)

I walked to the coach's door. Hearing the inner voice of my mother, I stood up straight. I adjusted my clip-on tie and rang the doorbell. This was my moment.

"Hi," I said when the coach came to the door. "I'm here from *The Bulletin.*"

He looked at me and looked at my notebook. "Well, uh, thanks for stopping by," he said, "but the other carrier came by last night to collect. I went ahead and paid him."

Thus did I arrive in big-league journalism. It was like warming up for your first major league baseball game and being mistaken for the bat boy. Fortunately, things got better.

Covering sports at a small-town daily was the hardest work I've done in journalism: six days a week, lots of nights, lots of weekends, lots of stale pizza.

On Fridays in the fall, I'd work from 6 a.m. to 2 p.m. to put together that afternoon's sports section. That night, I'd cover a game, come back to the office and take results of, say, two dozen other games over the phones with a handful of other sports nuts until about midnight. (The latter was easier said than done, especially with losing coaches, who had a tendency to "forget" to call. After a while, you learned what bars they frequented and had them paged. Our motto: *You can run, but you can't hide.*)

When the results were all in, about midnight, we'd start turning them into stories. We'd finish about 2 a.m., stuff down a few pancakes at an all-night restaurant and go home to catch a few hours sleep — less if we hung around to play football in the restaurant parking lot.

Then, at least for me and my assistant, it was back at 6 a.m. to edit stories, write headlines and design pages for that afternoon's paper. (At a sister paper in Eastern Oregon, the sports editor simply brought a sleeping bag on Friday nights and spent the night on the newsroom floor.)

The half dozen sports editors from the Intermountain League were spread out across Central and Eastern Oregon, a high-desert area as large as Georgia or Pennsylvania. In my five years as sports editor, I saw these people only once, at a makeshift "convention" we held in John Day, a place so small and rustic that you half-expected Marshall Dillon to poke his head in the restaurant during our plenary session on Selecting League All-Stars. Mostly, the sports editors communicated by phone and something called the "C" wire, a clackety-clack teletype that was to communication what a Model-T was to transportation.

A road trip in this league would often be five to seven hours long — one way. We rarely covered Friday night games on the road. But when we did, it would mean arriving back in Bend at 4 a.m. and having a story written by 6 a.m. And then, of course, designing the pages, copy editing other stories, writing headlines and checking pages until about noon.

Summers were more relaxing. A handful of us sports staffers would sit in the bleachers at Vince Genna Stadium, covering Bend's Class A minor league baseball team while the sun slipped behind the Three Sisters mountains to the west. Between pitches, we'd throw trivia questions to part-timers Rod Hanson and John Pritchett and watch them fight over them like sharks being tossed heads of halibut.

Hanson, a local high school history teacher, was The Natural, a guy who majored in baseball trivia and minored in the odd combination of Bible and '60s/'70s music. He won so many between-inning trivia contests that stadium officials banned him from competing; he didn't care, he'd just sit back and start rattling on about Ronald Reagan's six greatest sports movies or how only two people in the Bible have names starting with "F" (Felix and Festus), or how a former Mets pitcher once tried to burn down Rod's back fence.

Pritchett, fresh out of high school, was The Rookie, but could match Hanson on the most meaningless of minutia. Whenever he got down in the count, Pritchett would try diverting the theme from baseball to Eric Segall's *Love Story*, the first five pages of which he had completely memorized. ("What can you say about a twenty-five year-old girl who died? That she was beautiful. And brilliant. That she loved Mozart and Bach. The Beatles. And me ... .")

It was a wonderful life, particularly after Bend, which was affiliated with the Philadelphia Phillies, won the Northwest League championship in 1978. I was walking out of the clubhouse after the celebration when a small pack of autograph seekers spotted me.

"Hey, are you anybody?" one of them asked.

I couldn't lie. "Yeah, I'm somebody," I said, meaning that, yeah, I had a name and social security number.

"Cool," he said, and handed me a program. I signed half a dozen autographs that night, later wondering if those kids ever tried to figure out who I was and what position I played.

As *The Bulletin's* sports editor, I had unlimited freedom to create. I did a full-page feature on nothing but foul balls. I wrote a weekly column. On occasion, thanks to Bend's reputation as a vacation garden spot, I even got to interview some big-name athletes, including New York Giants star Y.A. Tittle, he of that famous photograph of the aging quarterback on his knees, without a helmet, blood coming from his nearly bald head. And, of course, Portland Trail Blazers star Maurice Lucas, he of that infamous interview in a moving station wagon in which, engrossed in a game of backgammon with a Blazers staffer, he never once looked up at me.

That's how it was being a sports editor for a 20,000-circulation paper: Just when you thought you were pretty important, you'd be reminded you weren't. Like the January night I was going to the bathroom in the locker room at half-time of a Bend High basketball game — only to have the team in the other room finish getting its pep talk and go back on the court, leaving me locked inside. I wound up climbing out a back window into the 25-degree cold and running around the school, where I had to show identification to convince the ticket-taker I was the paper's sports editor.

I took a lot of heat from my colleagues for that one, but not as much as another reporter took after he filled in for me while I was away for a few days. It was Masters weekend and the radio was reporting that a relative newcomer to professional golf, Spain's Seve Ballesteros, was the surprise leader.

Upon returning, I asked my assistant how everything had gone. "Super," he said. "I even saved our hide on a mistake The Associated Press made."

"What's that?" I asked.

"Oh, those bozos had 'S-E-V-E Ballesteros' in a story — left out the 'T.'"

My trusty assistant, of course, had the presence of mind to tell our readers that the dashing young Spaniard, *Steve* Ballesteros, was leading The Masters.

But such downers were more than offset by other aspects of my job, such as the tremendous pay: $150 a week for 60 to 70 hours of work. At first, I couldn't believe I was going to make that much for something so fun. Later, I realized fun didn't pay the rent.

My boss, Mr. Chandler, was known in newspaper circles as the last of the rough, gruff, small-town publishers. When I asked him for my first raise, I understood why.

"No," he said, leaning back in his chair and clipping his fingernails. He then proceeded to explain all the benefits I got as an employee of his company that didn't show up on that check, including free parking and the yearly company picnic at Shevlin Park.

"And there's the added benefit of living in beautiful Central Oregon," he said. "I like to think that just being able to see the Three Sisters mountains on your way to work is part of your compensation."

Great, I wanted to say, but try telling that to the guy at Green-Mindt Grocery who accepts only hard, cold cash for a quart of milk, not a peek at the South Sister.

After a while, Chandler softened up and gave me a couple of raises. But I realized it was time for a change. Chandler had long encouraged me to get out of sports; when the paper decided to begin its first-ever Sunday edition, he asked if I wanted to be its editor. I said yes and left my official sportswriting days behind.

Sometimes I miss those days. I would, in the years ahead, still cover an occasional sports event; while working for a Seattle-area paper, I covered the only college football game in history in which a field goal was disallowed because of excessive celebration on the part of a horse-drawn covered wagon.

Washington was playing Oklahoma in the Orange Bowl when the Sooners kicked a field goal in the final quarter to break a 14-all tie. An illegal procedure call nullified the kick, meaning Oklahoma would have to try again from five yards farther back. Meanwhile, though, the "The Sooner Schooner" was making a celebratory loop on the field. Chagrined, officials assessed Oklahoma a five-yard delay-of-game penalty. Washington blocked the subsequent field goal, the momentum shifted to the Huskies, and they went on to win 28-17.

It was perhaps the oddest moment in my journalistic career: standing in Miami, Florida, at about midnight, interviewing a college student dressed as a wagon-train boss about how he and his horses were being blamed for Oklahoma losing the Orange Bowl.

But for all that I would do in the years after my full-time stint in sports, there remained something special about those early days in Bend. When I left, my going-away present was not a gold watch, but a golf-ball retriever to pluck balls out of water holes.

An even better present was the memories I took with me of being a rookie in the hard, cold world of big-time journalism; of refereeing a 100-question trivia contest between Pritchett and Hanson whose outcome, 25 years later, is still in good-natured litigation; and of realizing I was finally somebody — and nobody at all.

Chasing the wind

When I was 14, I woke up one Saturday morning and felt compelled to wallpaper my room in color *Sports Illustrated* photographs — right then, right that moment, as if I were being called to fulfill some sort of latent decorating destiny.

So, almost like Richard Dreyfuss in *Close Encounters of the Third Kind* when he finds himself driven to create a mud-based scale model of Wyoming's Devils Tower in his living room, I began madly cutting out photographs from the two years' worth of magazines I'd saved. I took masking tape, cut one-inch strips, rolled them together, then stuck them to an old wooden snow ski that I'd bought at the Woodman's garage sale for 25 cents. My mother always wondered why I'd bought that ski — frankly, so did I — until this Saturday morning when I needed a 7-foot-long tape dispenser. Now we both knew.

You see, when I refer to "wallpapering," I don't mean that in a figurative sense. I mean that in an every-square-inch-except-the-ceiling sense. I mean that in a took-me-two-full-days-to-do-it sense. I mean that in a used-two-rolls-of-masking-tape sense.

In a single weekend and with my mother's blessing, I turned my room into a shrine to the publication that I very nearly worshipped:

Sports Illustrated. It was a tribute to what I believed to be the pinnacle of publishing. A magazine that embodied all that was good about sports. Above all, a magazine, I hoped, that my byline would someday grace.

They were all around me: hundreds and hundreds of pictures, creatively cropped and arranged. The images of photo masters such as Walter Iooss Jr. and Neil Leifer. Images such as the Colts' Johnny Unitas eyeing a receiver behind his single-barred face mask. Kansas City's Campy Campaneris fielding a grounder. The Celtics' Bill Russell soaring for a rebound. Runner Jim Ryun rounding a curve at the '68 Olympic Trials. Coach Vince Lombardi grinning that gap-toothed smile. Skater Peggy Flemming spinning. Baby-faced Jack Nicklaus looking like a muni player in one of those silly bucket hats. Dozens of cross-country skiers gliding across a Finnish meadow. Long jumper Bob Beamon leaping into history with a world-record jump that almost defied reason. An exhausted UCLA defensive back, Bob Stiles, being helped from the field. Ali landing a punch. Arnie sinking a putt. Doug Sanders wearing a gaudy golf outfit in which everything from shoes to hat was the color of the burnt peanuts you buy at 7-Eleven.

I'd been a subscriber since age 12 when my parents gave me the magazine as a Christmas gift. My friends all wanted to grow up and be Lou Brock or Elgin Baylor or Johnny Unitas. I wanted to grow up and be Frank DeFord or Mark Mulvoy or John Underwood, writers for *Sports Illustrated.*

I marveled at how these people could take me places and show me things and move me in ways unimaginable. At how the photos took me inside the games themselves, like being in an aquarium and seeing the fish up close. At how the artists filtered spring training or summer football camp — even a boat show — through their creative minds to offer images that said so much.

In the movie, *It's a Wonderful Life,* a young George Bailey is working at Mr. Gower's Drug Store when he pulls out a magazine and boasts to Mary Hatch that he's been nominated for membership in the National Geographic Society. He then goes on to tell her how someday he will explore the world.

That was me. Only in my scene, that was a *Sports Illustrated* in my back pocket and my dreams weren't of exploring Tahiti, the Coral Sea or the Fiji Islands, but of exploring the world of sports: athletes, games, stadiums. And having a story published in *Sports Illustrated,* I figured, would be my equivalent of discovering the lost ark of the covenant: the ultimate treasure.

My first attempt came on November 19, 1967. I was 13 and grieved that the magazine had given Oregon State only one measly paragraph after my beloved Beavers had knocked off O.J. Simpson and top-ranked USC, 3-0, so I wrote a letter to the editor.

"What does it take to get a decent article in your magazine besides being a Midwestern or Southern team or USC or UCLA?" I huffed with a hint of Northwest inferiority complex.

The magazine sent me a nice form letter thanking me for adding to the excitement of college football.

In 1971, having matured to an all-knowing 17-year-old, I wrote again, this time chastising Tennessee's athletic director for stating that long hair impedes athletic performance.

The magazine sent me a nice form letter thanking me for adding to the excitement of college athletics.

I went to college, became a newspaper sports editor and began freelancing on the side. In my early 20s, I wrote a can't-miss first-person piece on the travails of an athlete — me — whose past was so full of losing seasons that when my junior high football team tied a game 0-0 we celebrated with pizza.

The magazine sent me a form letter that said, in essence, to not give up my day job.

In 1987, I sent them a letter decrying Marv Marinovich's attempt to turn his son, Todd, into "roboquarterback." They didn't send me back a form letter. Instead, they printed my letter. I was thrilled. But when your dream is to write an article for a magazine, having your letter-to-the-editor run is a little like playing Class A ball in Lodi, California, instead of making it to Yankee Stadium.

Later that year, the idea hit me: I could write a piece for *Sports Illustrated* on the invention of the "Fosbury Flop" high jump style. It could run just before the 1988 Olympics, exactly 20 years after Oregon State's Dick Fosbury stunned the world with his then-wacky style by winning a gold medal in Mexico City.

I had grown up three miles from the foam pit where Fosbury had perfected his backwards style. I knew the history. This story had it all: A fresh angle. Info that wasn't common knowledge. A touch of humor. And timeliness. I fired off a query letter to *Sports Illustrated.* Weeks later, an editor wrote back. I was stunned.

She loved the idea. How would $1,250 with a $250 kill fee sound, she asked. For a guy who once made $35 a summer writing Little

League baseball results for a small-town daily, being offered $1,250 to write a single article for the king of all sports magazines was like being given the keys to Disneyland after spending your life teeter-tottering. And $250 even if the article were to be rejected? I'd never been promised such handsome compensation for possible failure; it was like being on "Let's Make a Deal" and knowing that even if you picked the wrong door, you'd still go home with a year's supply of Eskimo Pies.

Not that I planned on being rejected. This was my one — and, perhaps, only — chance. I signed the contract immediately and threw myself into the project. My wife and sons, then 9 and 6, didn't see much of me the next few months. Once home from my newspaper job, I was in my office, making phone calls and typing. Or at the Seattle Public Library, scanning microfilmed newspaper and magazine articles until, sickened by the motion, I thought I'd throw up all over 1968.

I talked to Fosbury's boyhood pals. Old coaches. College competitors. I drove 800 miles round trip to Ketchum, Idaho, where Fosbury lived, and spent an afternoon interviewing him; even wound up paying for two motel rooms for one night. (Don't ask.) Finally, I finished the article and sent it away. Weeks passed. Then came a letter from the *Sports Illustrated* editor. I was stunned.

The editor had rejected the story. Too much this, not enough that; I can't even remember what she didn't like about it. But if I wanted to redo the whole piece, she might — the word "might" stood out like the neon of a hospital emergency room sign — reconsider.

I was numb. It was a warm summer evening and I was home alone with the boys. The contractual letter had made it sound like such a done deal. I had had this fish securely in the boat; now I was looking at a letter that said three months of work wasn't good enough. A letter that said my two-decade-long dream wasn't going to come true after all. In my journal to my older son, Ryan, I wrote this at the time:

> A chance at the big time — gone. I cried. I didn't know what to say. Mom was gone. You and Jason didn't quite know what to do, so you went about your normal routine. Then, after about 10 minutes, you came over, threw your arms around me, hugged me and started sobbing. "Dad," you said, "I just feel so bad for you."

I refused to accept the rejection. I called another editor at *Sports Illustrated* in hopes that he would read the story and overrule her. By sheer will, I could get that story in the magazine. I could convince these people of the errors of their way. I could — "We don't do that around here," the editor said. End of conversation.

What now? Do I admit defeat or recast the whole story? I wallowed for days. Finally, I made my decision: I would rewrite the entire article. I spent two weeks reworking it, said a prayer and dropped it in the mailbox. I wasn't particularly hopeful. Weeks later, the editor wrote back. I was stunned.

She loved it. My revisions were just what she was looking for. It would run in a few weeks, in the September 12, 1988, issue, she said. I whooped for joy.

For three straight days, I rushed to the supermarket to see if the magazine had arrived. Finally, I saw it: The Chicago Bears' Jim Mc-Mahon was on the cover, eluding a would-be tackler. And I thought: Somewhere behind Jim McMahon is my article. After waiting nearly 25 years to fulfill this goal, my dream was unfolding. Everything around me seemed to freeze, as if the store scanners stopped beeping and the Muzak quit playing. I opened the magazine. I flipped the pages. My hands were sweaty. Suddenly, there it was: The lost ark of the covenant.

But a week later, I was in the supermarket when I did a double take: there on the magazine rack, where the Jim McMahon *Sports Illustrated* had been the week before, was a new *Sports Illustrated* with tennis player Steffi Graf on the cover.

I couldn't believe it. Just like that: I'm history.

More than a decade has passed since the day that article was published in *Sports Illustrated*. Back then the magazine was like a simple bungalow that invited you to come in and stay awhile and listen to some well-told stories. Today it is a multi-level mansion, a street-of-dreams special full of angles and angst. But if life changes, it also teaches. It took me nearly a decade to learn the *Sports Illustrated* lesson, not that I spent much time actually looking for it. It came to me in the summer of 1996, after my father had died.

Hours after learning of his death, I was standing in front of the house in which I'd grown up. The same street where I'd played touch football. The same house on which the tattered basketball hoop that my father had hung was still hanging, a slightly rusty legacy of the man who was no longer there.

I was feeling empty and lost and hurt. Then, suddenly, my 17-

year-old son, Ryan, was there. He put his arms around me and hugged me and said, "Dad, I don't want to lose you like you lost Grandpa."

In the end, what I learned was the difference between what lasts and what doesn't. At the memorial service for golfer Payne Stewart, who died in a plane crash at age 42, what people remembered about him wasn't so much his golf shots or flashy attire, but his bonds with those around him. Material dreams don't last; relationships become the legacy that does.

I'm thankful my article was published in *Sports Illustrated.* But it was only a temporary high. It was, as Ecclesiastes says so well, "a chasing after the wind."

What I'm really thankful for is a son who, on that summer night when his father learned his story had been rejected, hugged me, cried with me, and said, "Dad, I just feel so bad for you."

Because nine years later, on the day my father died, that same son hugged me and cried with me in much the same way, just because he hurt for me. And I was reminded how sad it would be if we spent our whole lives loving things that can't love us back.

The shoelace

He was a no-name kid lost amid big-name athletes, a 22-year-old runner from Atlanta named Tim Willis who was competing far from home. He was an 800-meter guy. And he was in Eugene, Oregon, on this mild June evening in 1993 to run in the USA/Mobil Track and Field Championships at the University of Oregon's Hayward Field.

Reporter's notebook in hand, I stood at trackside. Willis' race began. As the runners in the two-lap event spaced themselves out, Willis quickly fell to the back of the pack. After half a lap, he was about five yards behind the leaders. After a full lap, about 10.

Had this been Hollywood, Willis would have run the bell lap like an inspired sprinter, lunged at the finish line to win, and later found himself surrounded by reporters and autograph seekers. He would have been the hero of the day. And when he awoke the next morning at the Hilton, the newspaper left in front of his room would have been emblazoned with his photo.

Instead, Tim Willis finished dead last. His time, 2 minutes and 10 seconds, wouldn't have won most high school meets. I watched as he sat in the infield, putting on his sweats. Not far away, reporters and autograph seekers crowded around pentathlete Jackie Joyner-

Kersee.

Sometimes, courage lives in the shadows. On this night, at least, it did. On this night, it lived in the heart of a young man named Tim Willis. There is nothing particularly noteworthy, you see, in running 800 meters in 2 minutes and 10 seconds.

Unless you're running blind.

He was 10 when it happened: Coats' disease, a hemorrhaging of the retina. Within three years, Tim Willis' vision was completely gone. In junior high, he started wrestling, which required running. The high school cross-country coach saw him run and invited him to come out for the team.

Why not?

Willis learned to stay on course with the help of a shoestring tether he shared with a guide, who ran beside him. The guide would say something like, "Ditch coming up. Three, two, one, ditch!" Tim averaged about one fall per race, but nothing worse than skinned knees.

By the time he was a senior in high school, Willis was scoring points as one of his high school's top five runners. But with him now making a difference in team results, the Georgia High School Association ruled him ineligible to run. Being tethered to a guide, they said, gave him an advantage that other runners didn't have. It broke the rules.

Willis was crushed. But after the story ran on the front page of the *Atlanta Constitution,* calls of support for Willis poured in from around the country. *USA Today* picked up the story. Willis was on national TV. And the athletic association overturned its ruling.

Tim Willis ran on in the darkness.

On the day before his race in Eugene, I met Tim Willis at the university dorm he was staying in across from Hayward Field. Reporters generally ask the questions, but instead Willis led off with one for me. Would I be willing to drive him to the spot where distance runner Steve Prefontaine had died?

Minutes later, we were there, on Hendricks Hill just east of the University of Oregon campus. I watched as Willis's hands felt the contours of a rocky wall along a narrow, twisting lane. All was quiet, except for an occasional bird chirping and the distant whir of Interstate 5.

"Pre 5-30-75 RIP" someone had painted on the rock.

I talked of how Prefontaine had been my hero when I was a young runner. Willis talked of how even though Pre had died when Tim was 4 years old, the Oregon runner became his hero, too.

"What I admired about him was the way he could come back," Willis said. "After finishing fourth at Munich, a lot of people might have given up. He bounced back and set his sights on '76."

What I admired about Tim Willis was that he ran at all. Watching him race the next night, I was reminded that courage isn't measured with a stopwatch but in one's willingness to risk. And humility to trust.

We often find ourselves alone on that starting line. Unable to see. Blind to whatever lies ahead. Destined, it might seem, to fail.

Which is where faith comes into play. Faith is more than about running in the darkness, it's about being willing to trust someone else to lead us through that darkness.

It's about dropping our pride and, in humility, admitting we can't do it on our own.

It's about tethering ourselves to the God who longs to be our guide and letting Him lead.

Faith, it seems, is born of courage. It has nothing to do with the eyes. And, as Tim Willis taught me that summer night, everything to do with the heart.

When life is suddenly more serious more of the time, there is also more need for it to be fun at least some of the time. That's why my family will be at a college football game this weekend. We need it. And deserve it, too. Not like a New York fireman deserves it. Or a medic at the Pentagon. But enough.
— Thomas Boswell, *Washington Post* sports columnist, September, 2001.

5

The
Fan

The author's mom, Marolyn Welch Tarrant, once cheered on her son while wearing her 1942 Corvallis High rally outfit. (Warren Welch)

Belonging

One Saturday in October 1988, I sequestered myself in my Bellevue, Washington, rental home like a jury member in a cheap motel, refusing to allow myself to even go outside. I didn't want to talk to neighbors, watch television, listen to the radio or answer the phone. To do so was to risk having someone tell me what I didn't want to hear.

It was a long day of waiting. Of wondering. Of wishing. But I made it. Finally, at 11:30 p.m., and with my family fast asleep, I turned off all the lights in the living room, switched on the television and did it: watched a taped replay of that afternoon's Oregon-Washington football game from Eugene, Oregon, without knowing the outcome.

I felt a little bit like a guy in a cartoon I'd once seen — a middle-aged man, alone, roasting a hot dog over a campfire, with a caption that read something like: *Kevin Myers, self-employed, holds company picnic.*

But I also felt a little bit more sinister than Mr. Myers may have felt. As a diehard Duck fan living just outside of Seattle, home of the University of Washington, I felt like a Christian holding a one-man worship service in the former Soviet Union. I was surrounded by millions of Husky fans, whose team had beaten my beloved Ducks 11 of the previous 13 years and who looked upon us Quacker Backers with great suspicion, if not outright distaste.

Any moment, I figured, my KGB neighbor, Mr. Miller, a devout "Dawg" who might have seen the blue glow of the TV, could burst through the door, point something at me, and say: "Turn it off, Mr. Welch. I have a remote and I'm not afraid to use it."

But one's collegiate football allegiance can't be compromised by fear or runaway imaginations. Thus, I spent the next three hours in one of the strangest states of agony and ecstasy I've ever experienced — a full-grown man, smack in the middle of enemy territory, watching a televised football game in the middle of the night. Not only that, but watching a game in which, because of my sleeping family, I couldn't yell and scream when the Ducks scored or stomp and wail when they were scored upon.

It was, well, agonizingly awesome. Oregon, which usually plays Washington tough but squanders fourth-quarter leads and loses, didn't do that this time. The Ducks won, 17-14.

At first, I wanted to call some of my fellow Oregon fans from around the Northwest, but most of them, knowing the results since about 4:30 p.m., probably wouldn't have appreciated a 2:30 a.m. reminder call.

I thought momentarily of stepping outside the house and screaming the results to the folks in the cul-de-sac, but thought better of it, realizing that someday I might need to borrow a socket wrench from one of them or have someone pick up our mail while we were on vacation. So instead, I did the only thing I could do: stood on the couch, pumped my fists in the air, and loudly whispered staccato cheers like a machine-gun with a silencer. *Bob Welch, Duck fan, holds victory celebration.*

"Fan," I must remind you, is derived from the word "fanatic," which Webster defines as "frenzied; marked by excessive enthusiasm and often intense uncritical devotion" to something. A fan, we're told, is an "enthusiastic devotee."

I am a fan. Many people are fans. By that, I don't mean we're spectators; a fan is also a spectator but a spectator is not necessarily a fan. A spectator is someone who attends a sports event in a stadium or coliseum or gym. A fan, on the other hand, is someone like a Washington State friend of mine, Doug Mohney, who taught his parrot to say "Hate the Huskies."

What's more, a fair weather fan doesn't qualify as a bona fide fan.

Fair-weather fans show up for sunny home openers and bowl games and leave early in the fourth quarter so they can beat the traffic.

Real fans are like my friend, Scott Wynant, who, while living in California, ran up a $200 bill while having his brother in Oregon hold the radio up to the phone during a Duck football game. (This happened in the pre-Internet days before you could listen to such broadcasts nearly anywhere in the world.)

Real fans are like the Washington guy I once interviewed who lived out in the wilds of the Olympic Peninsula; one Saturday each May, he would drive his truck to the top of a nearby mountain just so he could get radio reception to the Husky's spring football game in Seattle.

Real fans are like Dorothy Kearns Goodwin, who, in her magnificent memoir, *Wait Till Next Year,* writes of growing up in the '50s in love with the Brooklyn Dodgers. While listening to each game on the radio — and keeping a complete scorebook — she came to believe that, though she was just one little girl, she somehow influenced the outcome of Dodgers games.

She once gave slump-ridden Gil Hodges a St. Christopher medal blessed by the Pope himself in hopes that it would help him begin hitting again. After all, she reasoned, St. Christopher was the patron saint of travel; perhaps the medal would help him "return home safely each time he went to bat."

At confession, she also revealed to a priest that she wished harm to opposing players, particularly New York Yankees players.

> "I wished harm to Allie Reynolds."
> "The Yankee pitcher? And how did you wish to harm him?"
> "I wanted him to break his arm."
> "And how often did you make this wish?"
> "Every night," I admitted, "before going to bed, in my prayers."
> "And there were others?"
> "Oh, yes," I admitted. "I wished that Robin Roberts of the Phillies would fall down the steps of his stoop, and that Richie Ashburn would break his hand."

Like Goodwin, I've always supposed that there's some sort of connection between my allegiance to the Oregon football team and the outcome of a game. I have this unsupportable theory that the Ducks play best when I'm in the stands and worst when I can't even catch a game on radio. I hatched this theory in the fall of 1988 when I went on a two-week trip to Haiti with a Christian medical team.

When I left, Oregon's football team was 6-1, ranked 20th in the nation and was talking Rose Bowl. When I returned, the team was 6-4, unranked and playing without their star quarterback, whose shoulder had been separated at almost the same time my plane touched down in Port-au-Prince. Rose Bowl? The Ducks lost their last five games to finish 6-6.

Of course, there have been exceptions to my theory that Oregon plays better if I'm in the stands. In 1997, I gave up the annual Oregon-Oregon State football game to attend a Family Life Conference with my wife, which scored big points with Sally. Ah, but pride goeth before a fall. The good news is the Ducks thwacked the Beavers 48-30; the bad news is that I still haven't been completely forgiven for sneaking in a radio and ear plug to catch an occasional score — ironically, during the segment on husband-wife communication.

Fandom, I've learned, can be taken too far; one Christmas Day, my extended family joined us in Eugene and, as Oregon fumbled away the Aloha Bowl to Colorado, I became a regular Grinch. And boorish fans at football games, who drink themselves into oblivion then turn into foul-mouthed 5-year-olds, are on the increase. (Bravo to Jennifer Haliski, who, in 2005, showed amazing courage after tiring of hearing a Washington State fan badmouth Cougar quarterbackk Alex Brink incessantly. She plopped down beside the guy, introduced herself as Brink's mother, which she was, and proceeded to ask the guy if he'd mind if she called the man's children some of the names she'd called her son. Stunned, he shut up in a hurry.)

But when kept in perspective — when your interest doesn't become worship or licence to berate people — being a fan is a fulfilling experience.

It connects you to something bigger than yourself. It allows you a shared experience with those around you; among my favorite fatherhood memories are of watching athletic events with my sons. And, of course, after a week of work deadlines, there's a certain devious pleasure in having the freedom to stand up and scream whenever you feel like it.

At times, of course, being a fan can complicate life. Though now a Duck, my boyhood is rooted in Beaver memories, the most memorable game I've witnessed being OSU's stunning 3-0 upset over O.J. Simpson and No. 1-ranked Southern California in 1967. My father and I sat together in the north end zone, rain falling, the field a sea of mud, the crowd dressed like a mass of steelhead fishermen.

Since becoming a born-again Duck fan at 18, the best game I've seen was in 1994, an Oregon-Washington battle that I watched from the 38-yard-line with my two sons.

Down 20-17 late in the game, Oregon found itself on its own 2-yard-line, facing 98 yards and the unsettling reality that in the four years he'd been the Duck quarterback, Danny O'Neil had never brought the team back to victory when they trailed in the second half, much less against a ninth-ranked team that had earlier in the season beaten Ohio State and stopped Miami's 58-game home winning streak. But on this day, O'Neil drove the Ducks 98 yards for a go-ahead touchdown.

Ah, but the Huskies countered with a drive of their own that was excruciating for Duck fans; with 1:04 left to go, Washington was poised for the go-ahead score on the Oregon eight-yard line with first down and a timeout remaining.

"That's it. They've got it. We're finished," said my older son, Ryan, almost in tears. I could barely look myself, but mumbled some fatherly line about not giving up till the game's over.

The crowd had turned quiet. Having Washington drooling at our goal line with a minute left was like facing a firing squad; the outcome was pretty much settled, it was only a matter of when.

Washington came to the line of scrimmage, ready to pull the trigger. Then it happened, a defensive effort that many consider the most incredible play in the century-long history of University of Oregon football.

Despite having pummeled Oregon on the ground to get to this point, the Huskies stunned everyone with a down-and-out pass to the shallow corner of the end zone. Oregon freshman defensive back Kenny Wheaton darted in front of the receiver at the three-yard-line, intercepted the pass and raced down the sidelines.

Most incredible sports moments last only a second or two — some not even that long — but as Wheaton passed the only Husky with a shot to tackle him and headed unchallenged to the end zone, this play seemed to last an eternity.

In the stands: bedlam. We were hooting and hollering and hugging people around us who we didn't even know. I grabbed my camera and started madly taking pictures, knowing that I had to preserve something from this day.

I've never experienced such an instantaneous reversal of emotions; later, for some reason, I kept thinking of the darkness-to-light line in "Amazing Grace": *I once was lost but now I'm found/Was blind but now I see.*

Sports, you see, aren't an extension of life as much as a microcosm of life. And as fans, you soon realize that you're more than a spectator. Win or lose, you're somehow part of it all.

Whether lost in the revelry of 44,159 fans in a stadium. Or alone in your living room at 2:30 in the morning.

Woman in the photo

W ho's the woman in the photo?" From time to time, visitors at
work will ask the question as they survey my surroundings, including the photograph on the wall of a woman in glasses — glasses
that look like those squint-eyed tail fins of the '62 Chevy my folks
once drove. She is middle-aged and is wearing a rally uniform with a
big "C" on the front of it .

One look at the picture and I can almost feel the November drizzle
on my neck as I awaited my moment of glory. This was it. In a few
seconds, the opposing kicker would pummel that pigskin and, as the
lone kick returner, I would gather it in my arms as if cradling history
itself, dodging, dancing and twisting up the sidelines while the crowd
roared its approval.

This was the start of of he 1972 Turkey Bowl, an annual gathering of teenage souls at Cloverland Park in Corvallis, Oregon. Never
mind that such games, at that very moment, were going on all over
the country on this Thanksgiving morning. Never mind that we were
a bunch of has-beens and never-would-bes, a motley collection of
back-from-college boys who, when posing for the annual postgame
photo, looked like a blend of loggers, hippies and the "before" example of a laundry-detergent commercial. Never mind that the "crowd"

consisted of five people, down a tad from previous years because our official photographer, my father, hadn't shown up yet.

In my vivid imagination, we were an important part of gridiron history, dating back to the days when nineteenth century New England boys would spend Thanksgiving Day kicking a blown-up pig's bladder through the streets. We were Jim Thorpe, George Gipp and the Four Horsemen of Notre Dame. We were Johnny Unitas, Joe Namath, Bart Starr and Terry Baker, the only player from our home-town college, Oregon State, to ever win a Heisman Trophy. We were the days before artificial turf and domed stadiums and uniforms that never got muddy.

We were suddenly distracted by some commotion on the side-line. "Hey, Welch, get a load of your mom," said a teammate, John "Woody" Woodman.

The words blindsided me like a Dick Butkus blitz. I didn't have time to consider what they might mean. I only knew that at age 18, when you're about to partake in a macho game of mud football, you don't want to hear a teammate say, "Hey, get a load of your mom."

I looked over at the sidelines in much the same way you might look at video footage of a man being gored by a bull on the streets of Pamplona: knowing you wouldn't like what you would see, but knowing you couldn't not look. And there she stood, my wonderful mother — adorned in her 1942 Corvallis High rally uniform.

What was she, nuts? Why did it have to be my mother? Why couldn't she be home doing what other mothers were doing on this morning: fixing a turkey or ironing a tablecloth or listening to Uncle Harry's story about passing his kidney stone? But, no, my mother, at age 44, was wearing a pleated skirt and a white turtleneck sweater with a giant "C" on it for Corvallis. My mother was leading the four others in "sis-boom-bah" cheers that hadn't emanated from a mega-phone since the days of the Roosevelt administration.

The crowd loved it. My teammates loved it. My opponents loved it.

I did not.

Sure, it was vintage Marolyn, the gregarious free spirit of Nor-wood Street, the woman who water-skied way beyond the legal age limit, fed seagulls leftover spaghetti, organized the annual neighbor-hood potluck and, at an OSU basketball banquet, hammed it up for a photo with a seven-foot center, Mel Counts. Why? Because she figured her son would think it was cool, of course.

But as I awaited the kickoff, I didn't want anyone to know we were related. The game began. As we played, I pretended not to hear her as she shouted her encouragement from the sideline. The game wore on. My team lost.

In years to come, we played three more Turkey Bowls at Cloverland Park. Then all but one of us left town to get jobs or hitchhike across the country or go to graduate school or get married and have children. Decades later, when I was 44 — the same age my mother was on that day she appointed herself the Turkey Bowl yell queen — I overheard one of my sons telling a friend I was, well, nuts.

I'm not sure exactly why he told his friends that. Maybe it was because one December, for our church's Christmas program, in front of 500 people at the Hult Center in Eugene, I wrapped myself in two 100-bulb strings of blinking Christmas lights and, extension cord trailing behind, walked on the blackened stage as the emcee.

Maybe it was because on my son Ryan's 16th birthday, when we couldn't get any service at a restaurant, I used my cell phone to politely call the dining-room manager and ask — as I watched her from 30 feet away — if I could please get menus at Table 23. (It worked.)

Maybe it was because at a huge outdoor Rose Bowl party for the University of Oregon, I wound up holding college classmate and professional golfer Peter Jacobsen's paper-plate lunch so he could be photographed with a friend of mine. And after he left, I instinctively took a picture of his half-eaten chicken. Why? Because my golf-crazy son would think it was cool, of course.

My mother knew then what I know now: The world needs laughter.

My mother knew then what I know now: Children need to be cheered on from the sidelines.

At 18, your vision is blurred. You don't realize that, right in front of you, you're being offered a gift that lots of kids are never given. But then you grow up and the scales fall off your eyes and you realize that your mom wasn't on those sidelines in the rain to call attention to herself or because she was a lush or because she wanted to embarrass you. She was there for one reason and one reason only: because she cared.

Time is a teacher. I heard those cheers, Ma. Every one. I cradle them deep inside and, in small, unseen ways, those cheers and the many I heard before that day helped me grow up feeling safe and significant in a world in which many children did not.

So anyway, that's the long version of the answer to the woman-in-the-photo question. Usually, I give the other version when people ask who it is.

"That," I say with a quiet pride, "is my mom."

Fenway magic

It was a blustery October morning, a Sunday that suggested football more than baseball. Cool. Cloudy. In Boston for some speaking engagements, I had walked a block from my hotel to check out the morning-after scene at Fenway Park.

A handful of diehards were already lining up for what might be the final game of the season, though their long faces weren't exactly etched with hope. Garbage was strewn everywhere. Torn-apart newspapers blew down Landsdowne Street behind Fenway's famous Green Monster wall.

The papers were day-old *Boston Globe* sports sections previewing the previous night's Red Sox-Yankees game. Down 2-0 in the 2004 American League Championship Series, Boston was trying desperately to stay alive against its much-hated rival. Instead, the Yankees had ripped the Red Sox 19-8, which, for all practical purposes, said to Red Sox fans, including late-comers like me: *It's over. Again.* For the 86nd consecutive autumn, since two years before Boston traded away Babe Ruth to the Yankees in 1920 to trigger what ultimately would be known as the "Curse of the Bambino," the Red Sox didn't look like they were going to win a World Series.

The Red Sox needed to win this league playoff just to get a shot at the National League champs and were down 3-0 in a best-of-seven series. Champagne had already been procured for the Yankee celebration, 10 cases of Great Western purchased by the visiting team's equipment manager. So hopeless was the situation that in the late innings of the previous night's massacre, two Red Sox fans had walked into a souvenir store across from Fenway and switched allegiences, buying Yankees hats. By game's end, barely 5,000 fans were still in the ballpark. "That was probably our worst game of the year," Red Sox General manager Theo Epstein would later say. "Including spring training."

And what hope was there for tonight? Dave Schilling, the Red Sox's star pitcher, was suffering from a torn tendon sheath in his ankle and was likely done for the year, regardless of what happened in this game. No major league baseball team had ever come back from a 3-0 deficit in a championship series to win four staight. In fact, in all of major professional sports leagues, only two of 236 teams had done so.

Those were the odds, history suggested: 2 in 236.

And just hours ago, Boston had given up 22 hits to the Yankees and lost by 11 runs — at home no less. And now faced an 8 o'clock win-or-die game against the same team.

In bull-fighting terms, the banderillas had already been stuck into the bull's neck, weakening him. Now, the matador merely needed to plunge the sword into the neck and it would be over.

The scene on Landsdowne Street was bleaker than an early Bob Dylan song. I had only one choice:

To find a ticket as fast as I could.

In nearly five decades of attending sports events, I hear a *Field of Dreams* voice whenever I have a desire to see a game and a lack of ticket through which to access that game: *If you want it, it will come.* Somewhere. Somehow. You'll find a ticket or tickets. Before the NCAA's 1984 championship basketball game in Seattle, the buzz in town was that you'd need close to $500 to nail a seat for the final game. Working for a Seattle-area paper at the time, I talked my boss into the company advancing me $50. I could find a ticket, I vowed, for no more than that. And did, within a half hour of my search.

You get tickets the same way I tell students in my university journalism classes that you get stories started: You start talking to people. You push on doors until one of them opens. You grovel.

You get a ticket because you want it badly enough to find one.

But unless you're very wealthy, you begin, as in car buying, with a limit. Mine was $75, about 50 percent more than I'd ever paid for an athletic event and about 200 percent more than my wife would probably want me to pay. And about half, I soon learned, of what most scalpers were asking.

Don't panic, I told myself. By now it was four hours before game time; plenty of time for scalpers to get antsy. The weather was cool. The Sox were colder than cod on ice. The hope of victory was frozen in the glacier-locked reality that the Sox, though teasing you with success, will ultimately fail. Huge favorites over the St. Louis Cardinals, they will still win find a way to lose the World Series (1946). Fourteen games ahead of the Yankees on July 20, they will blow the lead and lose a one-game playoff to the Yankees when Bucky Dent hits a three-run homer over the Green Monster (1978). One out from a World Series win, they will give up three runs in the last inning — with two outs no less — to lose to the Mets (1986).

And when they fail, they will break your heart, even if, like me, you've come to love them late. A Dodgers fan as a kid, I'd lost interest in Los Angeles — and, really, major-league baseball in general — until moving to Seattle in the mid-'80s. There, I tried to get serious about the Mariners, but baseball in the Kingdome had all the ambiance of a candlelight dinner in a Boeing hangar. We decided to be just good friends.

It wasn't until spring of 2001 when, though not even in the market for a new team, I found myself infatuated with the Red Sox. I had begun coming to Boston to do research on a book (*American Nightingale*) about the first nurse to die after the landings at Normandy, a nurse who'd grown up in nearby Roxbury. And so, not able to swing $200-a-night hotels while doing research at Boston University, I'd found the century-old, pie-shaped Hotel Buckminster ($110 a night), two blocks from Fenway.

Research by day; baseball by night. When Boston was in town, that became my daily routine. The book came out in June 2004 and now I was back promoting it, mainly to hospitals and nursing organizations. And had wound up at Fenway for the same reason Ray Kinsella comes to Fenway in *Field of Dreams*. I just sensed this was a game I needed to see.

Besides, even if the Red Sox were on life-support in these playoffs, this was Fenway Park. Babe Ruth played here. Ted Williams, in the last at-bat of his life, drove a 1-1 pitch into the right-centerfield bleachers for a home run.

This was the oldest major-league ballpark in America. This was history, a place that opened in 1912, the week the Titanic sank. This was sort of an outside Mac Court, University of Oregon's aging basketball arena. Small. Cramped. But a place where, for those who care to listen, the past whispers from every nook and cranny.

And I was in town with $98 in cash in my back pocket and a free evening.

Sure enough, I soon found a guy who had had a block of four tickets for $90 each. Limit? What limit? I pulled out my wallet. "I'll take one," I said.

"Gotta buy 'em as a block, pal," he said.

I'd like to believe God has more important things to do than broker baseball ticket deals; all I know is that shortly after I turned to walk away I heard the guy say, "Hey, pal."

I turned. Three young women were standing next to him. "We got three," he said. "You're our fourth."

We made the deal — when buying tickets from a scalper, I always feel naughty in a good sort of way — and I told the trio I'd see them at game time.

Is there a better feeling than having a high-demand ticket secure in your pocket just before a big game? Fans were starting to pour into Kenmore Square from cars, buses, taxis and the Boston "T" subway system. I ran into a couple of Red Sox diehards from my home state — I was wearing an Oregon sweatshirt — and took their photo to e-mail them later.

The skies had cleared. The place was coming alive. The Red Sox Stiltman was walking around with glove and mitt, firing up the Yawkey Street crowd. For the first time, you sensed — beyond the smell of steaming Fenway Franks — that there was hope in the air.

My three seatmates turned out to be Simmons College students and Red Sox diehards, the type of fans who, while swooning over Johnny Damon, also knew Kevin Millar's on-base percentage. "Yankee girls," as they called young New York fans, "were only in it for the fashion." They had been to the previous night's game and had tests in the morning, but couldn't say no.

We were sitting deep down the first base line, almost to the home run fence, and about 35 rows up. As I sometimes do at sports events,

I took a panoramic shots from left to right. The John Hancock Score-board said: October 17, 2004.

The game unfolded and, quickly, it was clear this was not going to be a 19-8 rout like the previous night's. The Yankees led 4-3 go-ing into the bottom of the ninth and on the mound for the Yankees was Manny Rivera, the best closer in post-season history. He threw pitches in October like FedEx delivered packages in December — fast, furious and consistently. And needed only three outs to add yet another chapter of futility for Red Sox fans.

Watching from upstairs in a box, we'd later learn, Boston CEO Larry Lucchino took out a notepad and began writing some thoughts for a post-game talk he would offer, about how it was a bitter pill to swallow but the Sox would double their efforts next year.

It was well after midnight. Millar walked and was replaced by pinch-runner Dave Roberts. Traditionally, Red Sox players steal bas-es with the regularity of Halley's Comet. But as fans tiptoed on the tightrope rope of demise, Roberts stole second base. The Sox were suddenly within a single of scoring a tieing run and at least sending the game into extra innings.

The hitter, Bill Mueller, let the count go to 1-1, then drilled a shot up the middle. Roberts scores with ease. Fenway went nuts.

I was simultaneously fist-pumping and shooting photographs.

Of course, the play had only prolonged Boston's life, not given the Sox victory. But in the bottom of the 12th, Manny Ramirez led off with a single. David Ortiz stepped to the plate and, on a 2-1 count, stroked a fastball in the Yankees bullpen. Game over. Bedlam erupted.

I started madly taking photographs, one of which showed the scoreboard and the time of day: 1:23 a.m. The game had taken 5 hours and 2 minutes to play. I took a shot of the Simmons girls, bundled in coats, hats in rally-cap position, screaming and hugging each other in a way that suggested it didn't really matter how they scored on those tests in a few hours, that this was one of those forever moments.

At the time, we had no idea what, in a broader context, this mo-ment would ultimately mean. This game would become the tipping point for the most extraordinary post-season comeback in the history of major-league baseball.

Now down 3 games to 1, the Red Sox would win two more to tie the series. Schilling, the pitcher with the bad ankle, would win Game Six with a gutsy effort — but only after an orthoepdic specialist created a makeshift sheath to keep his tendon in place, having hustled a human cadaver leg from the University of Massachusetts on which to practice this rare procedure.

In New York, the Red Sox would beat the Yankees in the deciding game, the seventh, and I would be back on the streets surrounding Fenway for the historic moment, watching masses of people, mainly young people, testing the limits of cops in riot gear.

They would then sweep the St. Louis Cardinals 4-0 in the World Series, never trailing for even a single inning, to officially end the "Curse of the Bambino." In the weeks afterward, baseball writers would call it the greatest playoff performance in the century-plus history of the game. And it started on that cold Sunday night in Fenway Park in a game that reminded me to never sell your ticket till you've seen the show.

After all, imagine how at least one Red Sox fan felt, the fan who sold his or her ticket to that scalper.

The scalper who sold that ticket to me.

A fan's favorite books

When, after more than four decades, the librarian handed me the book, I held it with reverence. You'd have thought it was a long-long family *Bible* unearthed from some musty trunk in the attic. Instead, it was the first sports book I'd ever read: *Shorty at the State Tournament.*

As sports literature goes, it isn't particularly impressive, full of exclamation marks and "Doggone-its." And, I confess, over the years, it wasn't as if I missed the book. Then, recently, I spoke at a fourth-grade class on the virtues of writing. In the question-answer session, a little girl asked me what my favorite books had been when I was her age.

I remembered it immediately. Remembered how, as a fourth-grader, I'd been swept into the magic of Danny Clearly's journey to make the South High basketball team. And the team's march toward — well, of course — the state basketball tournament.

Thanks to Google and the wonder of the interlibrary loan system, I had it in my hands in 10 days, this book that unfolded with the magic of night snow in a streetlight.

When I was a boy, other sports books enchanted me, including *The Sports Illustrated Book of the Olympic Games* (1967) and *The Story of Football* by Robert Leckie (1965). But it was *Shorty* that gently nudged me into writing about such games myself.

I know that soon after reading *Shorty* I had scratched out a story of my own. I remember little of the "book" I wrote, only that it started with a little boy on a cold winter morning bouncing a basketball from his house, across the frozen lawn, to his friend's house next door. Two little boys. One basketball. And, it turns out, a dream that should surprise nobody considering from whence my idea had come: to play in a state basketball tournament.

Such books stay with us, some on shelves, some only in our memories, all having taken us places, answered questions or touched ours hearts in ways that only later do we sometimes understand.

What follows is not the best sports books ever written — only my favorites. I confess to a fairly narrow definition of sports on this list; were I to include outdoors books, my Corvallis High classmate Jon Krakauer's *Into Thin Air* (1997) would certainly be on the list, along with *A River Runs Through It* by Norman Maclean (1976) and any of Patrick MacManus's zillion laugh-a-minute books, such as *Never Sniff a Gift Fish*. But I've stayed with competitive sports. So here they are, my 10 favorite sports books:

1. *The Boys of Summer* by Roger Kahn. (1971). Kahn's poetic book about the 1952-53 Brooklyn Dodgers is about the allure of sports and the inevitable — and often painful — letting go of sports. I bought the paperback, a tiny photo of Ebbets Field on the cover, for $1.57 as a high school senior and it's still with me more than three decades later. As a reporter for the *New York Herald Tribune*, Kahn writes of his covering the Dodgers in two seasons that they lost the World Series to the Yankees, and, more significantly, of returning to interview the players nearly two decades later. In sports, two realities are always spinning like the rubber disks of an automatic pitching machine: the story everybody sees — the game on the field — and the story beneath. *The Boys of Summer* was the first book that taught me this important lesson. It's the book that inspired me in the late 1980s to go back and interview members of my beloved 1967 Oregon State "Giant Killers" football team for a magazine story, knowing that mine was more than a story of football. Likewise, *Boys* is not so much a book about baseball but a book about people. About the passage of time. ("The older a man gets, the better a ball player he was when young, according to the watery eye of memory.") About life. And possibilities. "It was late March and day rose brisk and uncertain, with gusts suggesting January and flashes of sun promising June," the book begins. "In every way, a season of change had come." In *The Boys of Summer*, such seasons beckon us back in time, yet leave us with a bittersweet lesson: We can't stay.

2. *Bowerman and the Men of Oregon* by Kenny Moore (2006). No author I've read does a finer job than Moore of not only capturing the essence of the legendary track and field coach Bill Bowerman but of distance-running itself. Part of that is because he ran under Bowerman, finishing fourth in the 1972 Olympic Marathon in Munich; he lived on the landscape of which he writes and so understands it well. Part of that is because he is a gifted writer, his talents honed on the pages of *Sports Illustrated*. But part of it, too, is that Moore simply notices the nuances of the people, events and times around him like others do not. In that sense, he's *Chariots of Fire's* Aubrey Montague, the journalist-athlete who came to understand fellow runner Harold Abrahams perhaps better than Abrahams understood himself. Beyond the Bowerman basics — he coached 16 sub-four-minute milers at University of Oregon, was the "Father of Jogging" and invented the waffle-soled shoe that would help launch Nike — Moore understood the inner man. "Bowerman knew and loved and distrusted us as he had been known and loved and distrusted himself," he writes. I admit substantial bias; as an Oregonian and a runner myself beginning in the late '60s, I grew up in the distant shadows of the Bowerman mystique. But even accounting for that, Moore is Olympian in capturing an extraordinary man who left more of an imprint on distance-running than anyone who's lived.

3. *Beyond the Game: The Collected Sports Writing of Gary Smith* (2000). Anyone who's read *Sports Illustrated* over the years is familiar with Smith's stuff; his articles are the long, deep shots to the nether-regions of the ball park that few hitters ever reach. His articles are the ones that avoid top-of-the-article summarizations, relying, instead, on teases that 12 pages and a couple of misty eyes later, you're glad you dared to follow. "I've always had the feeling that the most compelling and significant story was the one occurring beyond the game — before it, after it, above it, or under it, deep in the furnace of the psyche," he writes in his preface. "Conventional journalism couldn't always carry me up to those rafters or down into those boiler rooms, so I had to break out of a few of my own little boxes, as well." He has done so splendidly. Nobody I've read gets into the heads of his sports subjects better than Gary Smith; he's part writer, part psycholgist. Nobody dares to push the limits like Gary Smith. Nobody uses repeated phrases with such effectiveness like Gary Smith. In a world of one-dimensional sportswriters, Smith gets to the depths you associate more closely with fine novelists. In "Damned Yankee," about a former catcher haunted by the past, Smith uses one simple photograph to introduce a story that will take us beyond the pixels, into the heart, soul and mind of tortured John Malangone. Smith is part-jock, part-psycholgist — and all-writer.

4. *Wait Till Next Year* by Doris Kearns Goodwin (1997). The baseball-laced memories of the Pulitzer Prize winner's childhood in 1950s New York are like summer ice cream. They take us all back to more innocent times. For someone who normally writes of headier things — her Pulitzer was for a biography, *No Ordinary Time*, on the Roosevelt years — Goodwin shifts seamlessly from politics to her childhood worship of the Brooklyn Dodgers: her keeping score, by radio to show her at-work father how the games had gone (back when baseball was played during the days) … her descriptions of each family's allegiance to Dodgers, Yankees or Giants (" … passed on from father to child, with the crucial moments in a team's history repeated like the liturgy of a church service.") … her relationship with her father, intricately tied to baseball. Delightful stuff, this. No book I've read so wonderfully captures childhood fandom like Goodwin's.

5. *Sea Biscuit: An American Legend* by Laura Hillenbrand (2001). Great authors can make you care about a subject that initially has no more appeal to you than Spam. Thus, did I find Hillenbrand drawing me — no equine fan — into a story about a 1930s race horse that captured the heart of a Depression-ridden nation. As an author who's written a biography, I appreciated Hillenbrand's indefatigable research. As a lover of words, I marveled at her descriptions: "Charles Howard had the feel of a gigantic onrushing machine: You had to either climb on or leap out of the way. He would sweep into a room, working a cigarette in his fingers, and people would trail him like pilot fish." And as a lover of sports, I was mesmerized by a story of an out-of-nowhere horse who takes us along for an amazing ride.

6. *Final Rounds* **by James Dodson (1996)**. A son takes his dying-of-cancer father to England and Scotland in the months before the man's death. Golf's cradle is the background for a book that's as much about fathers and sons — and how adulthood doesn't stop that relationship — as it is about clubs and golf courses. Writers of sports are often better at digging into the lives of others than their own, but Dodson proves a refreshing exception, daring to write of the father-son connection with candor. It's a moving book, particularly sad at the end, but nevertheless reminds us to connect with our fathers while we still have the chance.

7. *Golf in the Kingdom* **by Michael Murphy (1972)**. A weird-choice for a guy like me whose view of the universe is rooted in more traditional Judeo-Christian soil than the quirky stuff that grows the gorse of Murphy's Burningbush in Fife. But something about Shivas Irons, a mystical caddie-come-guru, beckoned me like an empty 10th tee at dusk. I just had to tee it up and play.

I wouldn't put much real-life stock in Irons' loopy philosophies, but as a book about golf, it's entertaining, insightful and intriguing. A spiritual masterpiece? Naw. But perhaps no author has gotten to the soul of golf like Murphy does through the imagination of his philosopher-poet Irons.

8. *The Tumult and the Shouting* **by Grantland Rice (1954)**. Sometimes failure leads us to riches we would have otherwise missed. In the spring of 1976, when, a month before graduation, I discovered I was one credit short, University of Oregon journalism professor Charles Duncan offered me grace: a one-credit class in the history of sportswriters.

Thus did I get to better understand Grantland Rice, he of the "Outlined against a blue-gray October sky …" lead about the 1924 Notre Dame team's "marvelous backfield." The book constitutes the last of the estimated 67 million words written by Rice; he completed this autobiography three weeks before his death in 1954, the year I was born. Like other sportswriters in the so-called "Golden Age of Sports," Rice succumbs to hero worship at times. But, then, who wouldn't at least be wide-eyed when writing about such folks as Jack Dempsey, Babe Ruth, Bobby Jones and Knute Rockne? It was Rice who, ahead of his times, defended the right of athletes to make a living as professionals, but also Rice who decried the warping influence

ing as professionals, but also Rice who decried the warping influence of big money in sports. And Rice who, in 1948, as a eulogy for Babe Ruth, wrote the immortal words about keeping sports in perspective:

> Upon the field of life
> the darkness gathers far and wide,
> the dream is done, the score is spun
> that stands forever in the guide.
> Nor victory, nor yet defeat
> is chalked against the player's name.
> But down the roll, the final scroll,
> shows only how he played the game.

9. *ESPN College Football Encyclopedia,* **edited by Michael MacCambridge (2005).** Every best-sports-book list should include at least one almanac, for numbers and trivia are to sports what the heart and lungs are to the body. If $1 was the least I paid for a book on this list (*The Tumult and the Shouting,* bought at a used book store), the $40 I shelled out for this encyclopedia was the most. And it was 20 percent off. But how could I resist? It is 1,629 pages long. Weighs 7 pounds and 1 ounce, the size of a small retaining-wall brick. But it was love at first skim: essays on college football. The result of every game — more than 111,000 — of every NCAA Division 1-A school. Fascinating factoids about each school. (Who knew that the Akron Zips were originally named after a popular pair of rubber overshoes, Zippers, made by B.F. Goodrich?) And it features a 16-page color centerfold showing the evolution of helmet designs for all major teams. It is the Swiss Army Knife of college football, a book with not only facts and visual flair, but also a slight attitude that says: *Yes, we know it's weird for a bunch of grown men to be debating who has the coolest college football uniforms, but who cares?*

Therein lies the wonder of sports: You can be as trivial as you want to be.

10. *Shorty at the State Tournament* **by C. Paul Jackson (1955).** You remember a first book like you remember a first kiss: not necessarily because it was the best or came from someone who you would wind up spending a lifetime with, but because it was the first. Context is everything. This is a book that reads like a sepiatone photo looks: old. And a touch schmaltzy, full of exclamations of "jeepers" and "doggone its." But it was a book written for young people half a cen-

tury ago. And, for all its mustiness, I found, skimming it once again, a
certain pang for the days when "doggone it" was as bad as it got.

Also receiving votes: *Last Days of Summer* by Steve Kluger
(1998), *SportsWorld* by Robert Lipsyte (1975), *The Curse of the
Bambino* by Dan Shaughnessy (1990), *Reversing the Curse* by Dan
Shaughnessy (2005), *Men at Work: The Craft of Baseball* by George
Will (1990), *The Legend of Bagger Vance* by Steve Pressfield (1995),
Golf: The Passion and the Challenge by Mark Mulvoy and Art
Spander (1977) and *Red Sox Journal: Year by Year & Day by Day*
with the Boston Red Sox since 1901 by John Snyder (2006).

A fan's favorite movies

Sports movies are like walking the Oregon beaches in search of sand dollars: They're rare to begin with and, usually when you do find one, it's broken. But every now and then you find the sand dollar still whole, glorious in its intricacy, simple and inspiring.

As opposed to, say, the sand dollar named *Caddyshack II, Happy Gilmore* or *The Replacements.*

I admit it: I'm a sentimentalist. I like a happy ending. I don't discount a sports movie just because, as you suspect in the first scene, the home team wins the championship in the last. But I also ask for some believability. (Unlike *Gus.*) I ask that the sports-action scenes actually look like sports-action scenes. (Unlike *The Natural*, in which Robert Redford manages to purposely hit a foul ball at a sportswriter — and hits a homer into a bank of outfield lights, triggering a fireworks display that makes New York City's Fourth of July show look like a handful of discount sparklers.) Finally, I ask that you offer an actual story as opposed to just a good-looking actor with a baseball mitt. (Unlike Kevin Costner in *For Love of the Game.*)

With such biases confessed, here are my 10 favorite sports movies:

1. *Hoosiers* (1986). Gene Hackman stars as coach of a Hickory

High basketball team (based on the 1954 Milan High team) in a blink-and-you-miss it Indiana town that does the impossible: wins a state championship. *Hoosiers* succeeds not because of the well-worn David-beats-Goliath theme but because every character — from a coach looking for redemption to an alcoholic father looking for worthiness to the town's favorite son looking for a sense of belonging — is chiseled from real stone. Sure, the movie has its cheesy moments — a manager-turned-player hits a game-winning free throw — but we allow such moments because *Hoosiers*, above all, teaches us to believe. In ourselves. In beating the odds. In the unredeemable. And because nearly every scene has some line that, years later, you remember. Among them: "I play, coach stays, he goes, I go." And "We're gonna run the picket fence at 'em. ... Boys, don't get caught watching the paint dry!" And "You did good, Pop. You did real good." And "I think you'll find these exact same measurements as our gym back in Hickory." And "Let's win this one for all the small schools that never had a chance to get here." And "... David put his hand in the bag and took out a stone and flung it, and it struck the Philistine in the head, and he fell to the ground. Amen." And "I love you guys."

2. *Chariots of Fire* (1981). Chariots is a triumphant trinity — alluring cinematography, a compelling story and an inspiring soundtrack.

At its core it is less about two runners preparing for the 1924 Olympics than about two men and their faiths. For Eric Liddell, a Christian, it is about his faith in God. For Harold Abrahams, a Jew, it is about his faith in himself.

Liddell's missionary sister insists his running is only getting in the way of his life's calling: to be a missionary. "I believe that God made me for a purpose, for China," he tells her. "But He also made me fast, and when I run I feel His pleasure."

Meanwhile, Abrahams is a man haunted by the subtleties of anti-Semitism, a man who runs not for God, but to prove something. To himself and to the world. "It's not the losing, Syb," he says to his girlfriend after Liddel has beaten him. "Eric Liddell's a fine man and a fine runner. It's me. After all that work, I lost, and now god knows what do I aim for?"

Chariots won the 1981 Academy Award for Best Picture, begging the question: Could such a simple, no-frills movie about two men's faith win today? Doubtful, unfortunately. Nevertheless, just as the soundtrack seemed to be played at every road run ever offered in the

the '80s, the movie stays with those of us for whom glitz and glamor often just get in the way of the deeper things.

3. *Rocky* (1976). Rocky is for every one of us out there who wanted, say, a book published but could wallpaper our office with rejection letters. Rocky Balboa (Sylvester Stallone) is a meat-factory worker and struggling boxer who — hey, it's the movies! — gets a shot at the big-time: a bout with heavyweight champion Apollo Creed.

It's about heart having more clout than brains, Rocky not being the sharpest knife in the drawer. But you gotta love a guy who, in his pre-fight conversation with girlfriend Adrian, says: "It really don't matter if I lose this fight. It really don't matter if this guy opens my head, either. 'Cause all I wanna do is go the distance. Nobody's ever gone the distance with Creed, and if I can go that distance, you see, and that bell rings and I'm still standin', I'm gonna know for the first time in my life, see, that I weren't just another bum from the neighborhood."

Of course, a good boxer knows when to say when — when to quit. If only the studios behind the Rocky series could have done the same instead of making so many sequels that we half-expected the run to end with *Rocky XVIII: Stallone vs. the Planet of the Apes.*

4. *Bang the Drum Slowly* (1973). Starring Robert De Niro, this movie about a dying major-league baseball player starts out like the Mississippi River, wide, flat and a tad boring, then funnels into an emotional waterfall. I'm not sure there's a more riveting scene in any sports movie as De Niro, a catcher, helplessly tries to find a pop-up while the camera catches the agony in slow motion.

5. *Caddyshack* (1980). Just so you don't think I'm a humorless one-trick pony when it comes to sports movies, here's an off-the-wall comedy that has little redeeming social value whatsoever, but whose lines still get repeated regularly when there's a jam-up on the seventh tee. On one level it's about golf, gophers, night-putting and a candy bar on the bottom of a swimming pool. On another level it's about, well, golf, gophers, night-putting and a candy bar on the bottom of a swimming pool.

Watch this "Cinderella story" for what it is: a cheesy golf comedy with a few scenes that need fast-forwarding and more than a few lines that'll stay in your system like maraschino cherries. Like what the Dalai Lama told Bill Murray after the caddy asks for a little something for the effort: "There won't be any money, but when you die, on your deathbed, you will receive total consciousness." So, says Murray, "I got that goin' for me, which is nice."

6. *Rudy* (1993). All things being equal, movies based on true stories mean more than those that aren't. Certainly, Rudy wasn't a mirror image of Rudy Ruettiger's life and times at Notre Dame; for example, the team did not actually lay their jerseys on Coach Dan Devine's desk as symbol of their unwillingness to play if Rudy didn't play. But that the 5-foot-6, 165-pound Ruettiger had a dream to play for Notre Dame, and ultimately did, is indisputable. Humor. Goose bumps. Realism. Rudy has it all, including Rudy's reply when asked if he was ready to play his first, and only, game. "I've been ready for this my whole life."

7. *Field of Dreams* (1989). Like the book *Golf in the Kingdom,* you'll have no fun with this movie unless you're willing to accept — in the spirit, of say, *It's a Wonderful Life* — that voices can come out of the sky and old ball players, including Shoeless Joe Jackson, can come out of a cornfield. Once you do, you're in for a wonderful film about following dreams. It's Iowa, Fenway and heaven all on the same stage.

8. *Cinderella Man* (2005). Russell Crowe and Renee Zellweger star in the story of James Braddock, a supposedly washed-up boxer who comes back to become a champion and an inspiration in the 1930s. It's *Rocky* without the "cut me, cut me" over-the-top stuff, a move that'll make grown men cry.

9. *A League of Their Own* (1992). American men are off to fight World War II and so the All American Pro Girls League steps into the box. Gina Davis is Dottie Hinson, an Oregon farm girl, who along with her sister, signs on with the Rockford Peaches. Madonna not only plays the field — literally, for a change — but co-wrote the theme song for the film, *This Used To Be My Playground,* and was nominated for a Golden Globe Award for it. And Tom Hanks, after putting on 30 pounds just for the role, is the perfect manager. It's hard to say which is the better scene, his morning-after urinal scene after a night on the town — suffice it to say he goes extra innings — or his insistence, amid an emotion upheaval among players that "there's no crying in baseball."

10. *Beach Runner* **(2002)**. Calling this a low-budget movie wouldn't be accurate. It's a no-budget movie. But, hey, my son Ryan wrote, produced and directed it — and filmed it in a weekend at our beach cabin on the Oregon Coast. It's the story of a high school athlete who leaves the promise of his father's auto repair business — a father played by me, my eyes seemingly Super-Glued shut — to pursue a dream of being a runner. More than that, it's a story about how anyone with a video camera and a vivid imagination can make a Top 10 Sports Movie list, though it helps if your father compiles that list.

Also receiving votes: *Sandlot* (1993), *The Endless Summer* (1966), *Brian's Song* (1971) and *The Rookie* (2002).

The Giant Killers

It was spring, the wrong season to be standing in a college football stadium, perhaps the wrong decade as well. For it was quiet, empty, lifeless, like a body without a soul. The stadium mirrored little of the mystique that I remembered from those autumn afternoons long ago, when my pal Woody and I would race our bikes down Arnold Way, buy 50-cent tickets and watch what we both knew was the greatest football team to ever don shoulder pads.

Later, I had returned to Parker Stadium at Oregon State University half-believing it would all be the same. Of course, it wasn't; twenty years is a long time. The checkerboard end zones were gone. A larger, more sophisticated scoreboard had replaced the one that once flashed the score above all scores: OSU 3, USC 0. The muddy field on which my beloved Beavers had beaten No. 1-ranked Southern California had been replaced by artificial turf.

As fans, we all have one team that stands out above the rest. For me, this was that team: The unheralded 1967 Oregon State football team that came out of nowhere to stun top-ranked Purdue 22-14, tie second-ranked UCLA 16-16, and beat top-ranked USC — with Heisman Trophy-winning tailback O.J. Simpson — with a lone field goal.

They were called the Giant Killers.

This was more than just one team beating the odds. It was, as one player would later say, "corn-fed boys who played with their hearts" defeating America's media darlings, a team from a state whose well-tanned governor, Ronald Reagan, watched glumly from the press box.

In the fall of 1967, a season ticket to OSU games cost $16. Simon and Garfunkel were singing about feelin' groovy. And America's favorite television show was "Andy Griffith." Once, through what I was sure was divine intervention, OSU's quarterback, Steve Preece, wound up having dinner at our house; his roommate was the son of some close family friends. I unsuccessfully lobbied my mother to frame the plate on which he'd eaten.

But everything changed after that season. Nothing would ever seem as simple. Author William Manchester labeled 1968 "the year everything went wrong." Drug use mushroomed. The Vietnam War grew uglier. Anti-war protests intensified. And Martin Luther King Jr. was assassinated.

Senator Bobby Kennedy came to Corvallis to campaign for the Democratic nomination for president; my mother took me to hear him speak in front of the courthouse. A few weeks later, he was dead, gunned down in Los Angeles.

Then, in the spring of 1969, four students from my community were driving back from a state tournament basketball game in Corvallis and were killed in a gruesome auto accident, and I realized that life wasn't as safe and certain as I'd thought.

I was going through a box of old newspapers one evening when I found it sandwiched between Neil Armstrong's moon walk and distance runner Steve Prefontaine's fatal car wreck: *Incredible OSU crumbles Troy.*

What had become of the players on this team, I wondered. At 33, I suddenly had the urge to know, the urge to write about them. *Northwest*, then the Sunday magazine at *The Oregonian* newspaper in Portland, was interested in the story so I embarked on a journey to find out. I drove hundreds of miles, interviewed dozens of players, scanned hundreds of feet of microfilm.

What did I find?

That heroes are best remembered in the context in which we first find them. That an athlete's toughest challenge is often learning to live after the cheering has stopped. And that no matter how high we put them on pedestals, athletes are, above all, human.

Most of the players who had come down the Parker Stadium ramp in 1967 were about 40 years old when I returned to interview them. And most had found success in the world; they were bringing up families, entrenched in jobs they liked, seemingly content with the past and the present.

But not all of them. Some stumbled. Some made poor choices. Some lost focus. In short, I found they were not the invincible Giant Killers I remembered from my youth.

I remember one player, wingback Donnie Summers, who was lost without the spotlight of football. No job, no relationships. He found nothing to fill the hole sports had filled and wound up as a bouncer in a bar, brawling, and drinking. On occasion, he'd stop by Parker Stadium and just stare and remember. He once wrote a poem that read, in part:

> If you pass by a stadium
> Some lonely night
> And hear a lonely voice calling
> Out old remembered plays ...
>
> Please don't interrupt until I have
> Raced across the field
> Weaving back and forth,
> Hurdling opposing tacklers with
> My imaginary football tucked
> Under my arm.

Athletes, it's been said, die two deaths — one when their career is over and one when their heart stops. It wasn't until he was 35 that the man accepted that first death, which freed him to live again.

A few of the players tried desperately to keep playing, bouncing around the NFL and Canadian Football leagues. But injuries and reality caught up; only one player had a substantial NFL career.

A few of the players built what, on the outside, looked to be ideal lives. One lived atop a hill, was a successful businessman, and had a wife and two teenage children. But divorce shattered his family.

A few of the players tried to replace the glory days with money. "I had the world by the tail," one told me. "At age 23, I didn't owe a dime, I had $10,000 to $15,000 in my bank account, and I was married. So what'd I do? I started dropping acid."

If some made poor choices, others had no choice at all. On the morning after OSU's win over USC, one player didn't have time to read the newspaper accounts of what is still considered the biggest victory in the school's century-plus football history. He was on a bus to an airport. His ultimate destination? Vietnam.

He came back with a Purple Heart after a Viet Cong soldier hurled a grenade while the man was on night patrol. A buddy to his side never made it out, but he did — unconscious, bleeding, his body full of shrapnel, his right eye missing.

A year later, in 1969, OSU players were warming up for spring practice when they saw a familiar-looking player emerge from the locker room, dressed in pads, ready to play. It was the Vietnam vet.

In a made-for-TV movie, the man would have returned gallantly to grandeur. But in real life, many Vietnam vets learned you can't go home again — and, in a sense, this man was one of them. With his step slowed and his vision impaired, he never played another down of football at Oregon State.

It's now been more than a decade since I revisited the Giant Killers that fall of 1987. I was skimming the newspaper obits recently when I saw the photo: it was him, the player who had gone off to Vietnam. At age 51, he had succumbed to Lou Gehrig's disease. He was believed to be the first member of the Giant Killers team to die.

I stared at the picture and read the obit once, then again. It didn't seem possible. These guys don't die. These guys are all 19 and 20 years old. They beat all odds. They're the Giant Killers.

But, then, maybe that was the latent lesson from revisiting the heroes of my past: That not only is life not a made-for-TV movie, but the good guy doesn't always win in the end.

A decade before, I had learned that my heroes were human — and unprotected by helmets, shoulder pads and youth, not nearly as indestructible as they were through the eyes of a 13-year-old. But until now, I'd never considered the ultimate Goliath: death.

Blaise Pascal, the 17th-century French religious philosopher, believed that we're each born with a longing in our hearts — a longing destined to be filled with something, or someone. It is, he contended, a God-shaped vacuum.

Athletics, I believe, can neatly fill that vacuum. For a while.

The adulation of others, I believe, can neatly fill that vacuum. For a while.

Youth, I believe, can neatly fill that vacuum. For a while.

But I don't think anything ever fits — and keeps fitting — like the One whose perfect shape is missing, the One who promises to guide us through the changes of life, the One through whom we can slay even the ultimate Goliath.

On that day I'd returned to Parker Stadium, the campus chimes had drawn me back to the way it had been. After hearing those bells, I remembered my father and me sitting in those end zone seats. When the USC game was over, when Goliath finally fell, we rushed the muddy field and frolicked with a bunch of players who never thought they'd ever wake from this dream and go off to war or wind up in drug rehab or be served divorce papers or die.

In some ways, I wish I could freeze-frame the fall of 1967, for it had a purity about it that's been polluted in the decades since by a culture increasingly bent on greed. By the painful realization that life buffets even the strong. And by the inevitable winds of change.

Since the fall of '67, everything had changed — and nothing had changed at all. I left the stadium. In the campus quad, the Alpha Phis were selling Candy Grams. As I drove down Arnold Way, two boys on bikes glided toward the campus and, for a moment, I watched them in my rearview mirror.

Split decision

It was a short article on an inside sports page in the summer of 2006: Jay Locey, who had led Linfield College to the NCAA Division III football championship, would be joining the staff at his alma mater, Oregon State. He would be the Beavers' top assistant, coaching running backs and tight ends.

I reveled in the news. And yet also knew it would only further complicate my neurotic life as a college football fan.

You see, I spent the first 18 years of my life as a Beaver believer before, as some of my Corvallis friends still remind me more than 30 years later, "going over to the dark side" after high school. My grandfather attended Oregon State. My grandmother worked at Oregon State. My mother and father attended Oregon State and later worked for the university. Many of my friends would be attending Oregon State. Most of the adults in our neighborhood worked at Oregon State.

But wanting a degree in journalism, a program OSU did not have, I enrolled at Oregon and, despite my orange-and-black upbringing, was forevermore a Duck.

Sort of.

The problem is that even though I'm clear about whom I root for on the last weekend in November, I cannot change the fact that I was rooted in the soggy soils of Beaverville. And have familial and friendship ties to Oregon State that are forever reminding me of my "double life."

Example: Jay Locey was the best man at my wedding. A guy I've hiked and climbed mountains with. A guy I've played a magical game of one-on-one ice hockey with on the Cascades' Devils Lake. A guy I've cheered on since he started his coaching career, scouring the seven-point-type football scores in the Sunday paper each fall to see how Linfield, and Locey, had done.

But now among his chief goals — indeed, much of what will help him maintain his job at OSU — will be to thwart my beloved Ducks.

How do I deal with that?

Let me ratchet down how this rivalry tears at my emotional being: Besides being a Ducks season-ticket holder and having missed only a few home games since moving to Eugene in 1989, I've recently gotten to know a neighbor of mine, John Neal, who is Oregon's defensive backs coach. I really like the guy. In fact, after we had coffee one day, I thought: This guy has a great heart for not only the game of football, but also for the guys he coaches. He's a people person. He cares not only about developing football players, but about young men developing a sense of responsibility, compassion and drive. He reminds me of Jay Locey.

But get this: Among his chief goals — indeed, much of what will help him maintain his job at Oregon — will be to thwart Locey's beloved Beavers. More specifically, Neal's defensive backs will be trying to get the best of Locey's tight ends and running backs.

Now you understand how, when it comes to Civil War week, I'm like the speaker at the national schizophrenia convention who steps to the podium and says, "I'm so happy to be with you here today — or am I?"

Civil War week is always the best week of the year for me — or is it?

You see, I'm bi-collegial. Every fall, I want the Beavers to win every game but one. I want them to finish second in the nation. I want them to enjoy great success, just not quite as much success as Oregon.

Ah, but it's never that simple. Just when I grow comfortable with my Duckness — I walk like a Duck, I talk like a Duck, so I must be a Duck— out pops my inner child, and he's wearing a Benny Beaver sweatshirt.

I was born about a mile from Parker Stadium. The walls in my room were painted orange — my choice — and adorned with game programs bearing the likes of Beavers Jack "Mad Dog" O'Billovich and Bill "Earthquake" Enyart.

The Oregon State campus was my second home. After riding our Schwinns across town, we played football in the same stadium where the 1967 Giant Killers stunned top-ranked USC 3-0. And shot hoops in Gill Coliseum, always one step ahead of The Mad Janitor.

I played Wiffle ball and football with Mike Riley, who grew up to become head football coach at OSU. On my Tudor Tru-Action electronic football game, Oregon State won 439 straight Rose Bowls. And, of course, routinely thumped those dastardly Ducks.

Like many Corvallisites, I hated the UO. It was that loosey-goosey liberal arts school — my goodness, our coach, Dee Andros, had fought at Iwo Jima! — where students played football only when they weren't throwing Molotov cocktails or reading all that ryhme-less poetry.

The only good thing to come out of Eugene in the '60s, I figured, was "Captain Shipwreck," a KVAL cartoon show that my Cub Scout den once appeared on.

But then, like Paul on the road to Damascus, I saw the light — only I was on the road to Corvallis, after attending a Duck Preview week-end. It was February of my senior year of high school, 1972. And, as if blindsided by the linebacker of bitter truth, I realized something: I had to be a Duck.

What prompted the turnaround was my mother's insistence that if I was going to be a journalist, I needed the UO's School of Journalism. But for me, it went deeper than that. Way deeper. It was my latent realization that UO athletics had a certain class that OSU lacked: Steve Prefontaine and that shaggy hair. The Afro Duck decals. And running back Bobby Moore (later Ahmad Rashad) and the cool way he taped his shoes and pulled up his socks so high.

Word spread that I'd sold my soul to the tie-dyed devil. Oregon State was the straight-laced agricultural and engineering school where kids from, say, Hermiston came to revel in Phi Delt dances and Dad's Weekend; Oregon was Berkeley North, a bunch of glassy-eyed hippies whose idea of a good time was a good ROTC bombing.

Growing up in Corvallis and not going to OSU was like growing up in Coalville, West Virginia, and not staying to work in the mines.

My life got complicated as I tried to live in two different worlds. A week before leaving for college, I fell in love with the daughter of an OSU professor; she, of course, would go to OSU. For three years, I spent weekdays in Eugene and weekends in Corvallis.

As a born-again Duck, I wound up in all sorts of other weird predicaments, the worst of which involved Locey. It was Civil War Day 1975. I was sports editor of the *Oregon Daily Emerald,* the UO student newspaper. And Locey, the guy I'd cheered on as a classmate at Corvallis High, was a defensive back for Oregon State. In fact, as I watched from the Autzen Stadium pressbox in dismay/utter joy, Locey was racing 94 yards down the sidelines for a touchdown after intercepting a pass. Three months earlier, the guy, as my best man, had been helping adjust my bow tie before I took the wedding plunge. Now, here he was, coming to "our house" with a 94-yard "welcome present." After the game, which Oregon wound up winning, Locey came to our apartment. He couldn't really vent. We couldn't really celebrate. It was less fun than a one-person Twister party.

Such angst has dogged me for decades. Take the 1998 Civil War, for example: When time expired with Oregon State ahead, I resolved I could live with that. Oregon would still be going to a bowl game. The Beaver win would invigorate what had become a lifeless rivalry.

It was good for my old Wiffle-ball buddy, Mike Riley, who was now head coach at OSU, and for all of my Beaver relatives and friends.

But when officials announced that the game wasn't over because of a penalty on OSU, I thrust my arm in the air. Yes! The Ducks still had a chance

Then the Beavers scored to win in overtime. No!

I was crushed, elated, thrilled, bummed — a tangled mess of orange and black and green and yellow, the emotional colors bleeding together like that hideous grayish black-brown concotion school kids come up when mixing all their watercolor paints together.

It would get worse. Besides being casual friends with Mike Riley and his wife Dee, we're close with a couple from San Diego, Mike and Nicole Yorkey, who had become the Riley's closest friends when Mike took the San Diego Chargers job in 2001. Things didn't work out for Riley in San Diego, so he had returned to coach at OSU in 2003. And the day after Oregon's 2003 win over Oregon State, a game which Yorkey — staying with the Rileys — had flown up to see, he called us. Dee Riley would be driving him from Corvallis to our house in Eugene; he was spending the night with us before taking a flight home the next day.

Oh my gosh! I raced outside and took down our Duck banner; didn't want it to look like I was rubbing it in.

And so, an hour later, there was the wife of the rival coach whose team my Ducks had thwarted the previous day in our state's biggest athletic event of the year. There was Dee Riley getting a tour of a house splashed with green and yellow, with photos of my sons and I rooting on the Ducks, the cheers from the previous day all but still gyrating off the walls. It was like Custer's wife touring the Indians' camp the day after the battle. I felt terrible for her.

But she was a touch of class, joking lightly about the results while engaging my wife in more significant conversations about their common interest in vintage plates hung on the wall — and, in fact, accepting one as a gift from Sally.

She would be feeling considerably better a year later, the day after Oregon State thwacked Oregon 50-21. It was the most points a team had scored in the 108 games that had been played between the two teams.

On the day after that game, Sally and I drove to Corvallis to see the Rileys and Yorkeys, who had again come up from San Diego for the game. In the spirit of honoring Riley, I wore a bright orange blazer I'd won at a white elephant Christmas exchange at our church, looking a little like a well-dressed ODOT worker with a badly forced smile. Everywhere we went, Beaver fans were congratulating the Rileys. Slapping Mike on the back. Talking about the game. I felt good for them — and terrible for me.

But so it goes. That night, Sally and I returned home. I hung up the orange jacket, placing it on the far right side of a closet liberally sprinkled with green and yellow. Some Duck fans have criticized me as a turncoat, less than a true Oregon fan because I still have this touch of Beaver in me.

So be it. I love college sports. I love rooting for my alma mater. I love the elation of beating one's rivals. But when it all becomes more important than people, we've gone too far.

Thus, for my celebration of life someday, I've requested that the pianist opening the service begin with the Oregon State fight song, segue into "Mighty Oregon" and then into an array of songs that speak of the far more important things in life, like the God I've served. And the friends and family I've been surrounded with.

Regardless of what color jackets they wear.

The impossible dream

And David put his hand in his bag, and took thence a stone, and slang it, and smote the Philistine in his forehead, that the stone sunk into his forehead; and he fell upon his face to the earth.
— 1 Samuel 17:49 (KJV)

I had just walked in from coaching a Saturday morning soccer game and was still numb from a typical Northwest drizzle when my wife handed me the phone. All I wanted was a hot shower and an afternoon to relax.

"It's Johnny U," she said — not to be confused with *the* Johnny U, the Baltimore Colts quarterback, Johnny Unitas. My friend John Mills had inherited the "Johnny U" moniker back when we were growing up in Corvallis, Oregon — home of Oregon State University — because he not only wore geeky black high-tops like his hero but, like Unitas, could throw a football as if it were shot from a cannon.

Like me, Johnny U had taken a job in the Seattle area and now here he was, 13 years after our high school days, asking me to go watch lowly Oregon State get utterly humiliated by the Washington Huskies in a downpour surrounded by 60,000 fans wearing purple and gold and singing their unofficial school fight song, "Tequila," after each of their team's 12 touchdowns.

"You gotta be kidding," I said. "Have you looked outside?"

"Bobby, this is the day. This is the Beavers' day. I feel it."

"Johnny, the Beavers are 37-point underdogs. I don't feel it."

"Trust me."

I had read the sports page that morning. It was October 19, 1985, and Oregon State hadn't scored a touchdown since September 21. In their last two games, OSU had lost by a combined score of 97-0. The Beavers hadn't beaten the Huskies in 11 years. They had won only one road game in the last seven years. They were on a four-game losing streak.

"Oregon State," quipped one sportswriter, "is college football's get-well card." A TV station had shown an old film clip of Knute Rockne, the legendary Notre Dame coach, and said not even he could inspire the Beavers to victory. The 37-point margin was a joke, a Seattle sportscaster said. "It should be more like 70."

OSU was starting an untested freshman at quarterback. What's more, its only real offensive threat, flanker Reggie Bynum, had a bad ankle and wouldn't play.

The Husky Machine, meanwhile, was starting to roll; Washington had won four games in a row after going 11-1 the previous year and beating Oklahoma in the Orange Bowl.

The last time Oregon State had been to a bowl game, I was learning fractions at Garfield Elementary School. The last time OSU had had a winning season, 1970, not only were the players on its current team not born, but those players' parents were battling pimples and getting their learner's permits.

"Mills," I said, "It's gonna be ugly."

"Trust me."

"I'm already soaked. I've been coaching soccer."

"The tickets are free."

"The traffic. I'll get stuck on the floating bridge."

"Bobby, you won't regret it."

I looked at my wife with pleading eyes that said: Tell me I can't go. Frown hard, as if you want nothing more than for me to stick around. Ask me to clean the gutter sludge; I'd be honored to — and will gladly tackle the shower grout when I'm through, free of charge.

Instead, she looked at me with selfless eyes that said: Go, with my full blessing, and have fun.

I just stood there, saying nothing. Finally, I mumbled "OK" and started to gather my rain gear with the solemnity of a man going to a funeral.

When one of our cats used to catch a squirrel, it would often toy with the almost-dead animal before going in for the kill. That's what was happening at Husky Stadium in the third quarter on this drizzly October day in 1985.

An Oregon State defensive back had intercepted a pass in the end zone to stop one Husky touchdown threat. A botched snap from center by Chris Chandler — a guy who would one day go on to quarterback the Atlanta Falcons in the Super Bowl — had cost the Huskies an almost sure field goal. And another drive had stalled at the OSU 3 yard-line.

Still, Washington was leading 17-14 and had the ball first and goal on the OSU one yard-line. Four chances to go 36 inches; pretty good odds for an offense. This was it. This was the cat finally giving notice: Game over.

But after failing twice to score up the middle, Washington fumbled on third down and the Beavers recovered. Husky fans started doing something Husky fans rarely do: booing their own team. A sprinkling of fans in orange and black, including Johnny U and I, went nuts.

As we watched from our end-zone seats, we quietly basked in the new-found respect the Husky fans seemed to be according us. Losing to the Huskies by only a field goal would mean we could walk out of the stadium with heads held high.

The game wore on. Washington managed a field goal in the fourth quarter to make it 20-14 and, later, with just under two minutes left, prepared to punt from its own 20 yard-line, right in front of us.

I always remember the play in slow motion: defensive end Andre Todd bursting through the line on the right side … the punter receiving the snap from center … Todd smothering the punt, the ball caroming off him into the OSU end zone, bouncing around like a leather lottery ticket, awaiting the lucky taker … OSU's Lavance Northington swooping in and pouncing on the ball to tie the game 20-20 … Oregon State's players piling on the two heroes in celebration.

Moments later, Jim Nielsen's PAT kick sailed through the up-rights. The scoreboard showed 21-20, a score that would be on the board at game's end and seared into the memories of Beaver Believers forever.

"Hey, thanks for the ticket," I said to Johnny U as we headed to the parking lot.

"What'd I tell you, Bobby? You gotta trust me."

Washington would go on to win the Freedom Bowl that year. Oregon State, meanwhile, would go on to lose its next eight games. But every now and then, when looking for socks in a dresser drawer, I come across an orange and black "I Was There" button commemorating the 1985 victory, and I'm reminded of a truth that I've employed often since that rainy Saturday afternoon in Seattle:

Ignore what the so-called experts say. And dream the impossible dream.

I experienced that night what I have experienced many times since: the absolute pleasure that comes from prolonging the winning feeling by reliving the game, first with the scorebook, then with the wrap-up on the radio, and finally, once I learned about printed box scores, with the newspaper accounts the next day. But what I remember most is sitting at Ebbets Field for the first time, with my scoreboard on my lap and my father at my side.

— Doris Kearns Goodwin in *Wait Till Next Year*

6

The
Father

The author with sons, Ryan, left, and Jason following the 2005 Turkey Bowl in Eugene. (Sally Welch)

Sandlot journal

My father gave it to me when I was a young man, a small book the size of a pocket ledger. It was written and illustrated by a man named Will Adams, a journal chronicling two sandlot baseball teams that, as a teenager a century ago, he played on in northeast Portland. It's dated April 10, 1905.

Few people have ever read it, but I'm among those few. Will Adams, you see, was my grandfather.

I wish he could have known how much his words and drawings and self-invented box-score system have meant to me. But he died when I was 8, never realizing the legacy that would be handed down to me.

He played for two teams, one a school team — Williams Avenue School, just north of today's Rose Garden area today — and the Albina Tigers, a summer team.

Those were the days of thick-handled, think-barreled bats and mitts that weren't much more than padded garden gloves. In that decade, Honus Wagner set hitting records that would stand for four decades. The hot dog was invented. "Take Me Out to the Ball Game" was written. The World Series began. And Ty Cobb — two years older than my grandfather — left the fields of Georgia to play semipro baseball for $50 a month, carrying with him a pocketful of change and an edict from his father: "Don't come home a failure."

According to the baseball journal, my grandfather occasionally pitched but mainly played second base—the same position I played as a youth and the same position my two sons have played extensively. He also was team statistician and, judging from the journal, held that oh-so-rare position: team artist.

He would play a game, compile his own box score and draw sketches of teammates playing in baggy white uniforms with hats that made them look like police officers. His box scores were like none I've ever seen:

1 = scored

X = died on base

0 = made a good hit but was put out on base.

My grandfather finished the 1905 season with nine runs scored, three DOBs and 14 MAGHBWPOOBs.

"I pitched the first three innings," reads one entry. "Good many errors on both sides. I made the only score in the last by knocking a home run. A poor game without any double plays or science of any kind." Another: "Teachers and half the school were up to see the game. Two cops tried to fire us off but after same pursuasian (my spelling deficiencies, this suggests, are genetic) they said we might finish the game."

Reading the journal and looking at the often-comical illustrations, it was easy to imagine Will Adams' life neatly wrapped in nine-inning innocence. But when the yellowed newspaper clippings slipped out from the back pages, reality slid home, cleats high. The headline is: *Mrs. Welch's Serious Charges.* The story reads:

> Luzetta L. Welch has made application for divorce from William J. Welch, in the state circuit court. Cruel treatment is charged, and Laura Trabaunt is named as co-respondent. The plaintiff, as specific acts, states that the defendant on one occasion threatened to throw her out the window of their house; at another time she says he choked her, and once claims that he beat and otherwise abused her. She also alleges that he will not let her see her child.

The plaintiff in this court case was my great-grandmother. The child was my grandfather, Will Adams, who was seven at the time his parents' marital land mine exploded. Laura Trauant, we can assume, was the "other woman." I hate to imagine what "otherwise abused her" might have meant.

For all that he would accomplish in his 74 years, my grandfather's greatest triumph may well have been overcoming the very man who helped give him life. For his father was an alcoholic, an adulterer and a man whose family paid the price for his anger. (Interestingly, one of Will's drawings in the book shows a small child with a baseball hat being spanked by an unkempt, heavy-bearded man who scowls as he swats. "Say!!" the caption says. "You'se too small and little.") After his parents divorced, my grandfather was brought up by a stepfather, a Mr. Adams, whose name he took.

Generations of pain often repeat, the psychologists tell us now, but Will Adams did not repeat his past. He was imaginative, artistic and slightly mischievous. He and his pals — guys nicknamed Happy, Gus and Woozy, according to the journal — published their own neighborhood newspaper called the *Hooligan Gazette*. And they played baseball. Lots of sandlot baseball.

"The Albina Tigers and the Lower Albina team played a nine inning draw Sunday morning, each team making 7 runs," said one newspaper clipping in the journal. "As the Lower Albinas refused to play it out, the umpire decided in favor of the Tigers." (I take pride in knowing Will Adams was on the team that wanted to keep playing.)

In one sketch, he shows a first baseman reaching for a high throw. (Caption: "Harry always was a natural born reacher." Another, after an 8-1 Albina win, shows two feet sticking out of a grave, a shovel stuck in the ground. (Caption: "Put away.")

At season's end, he drew a player walking off, bags packed, in an apparent retreat to what my father always said was his father's real summer passion, camping. (Caption: "Back to the woods.") On the next page: A finely sketched close-up of a rose. (Caption: "We have rose colored hopes for the future.")

After a traumatic childhood, I believe Will Adams' future did get rosier. In fact, he became known as "Whistlin' Willie" because everywhere he went, he whistled. He met my grandmother. He became a father to my father. And though I remember only one memory of the man — buying me a candy watermelon at Arch Cape while I was visiting at their Cannon Beach cabin — he has become more real to me now than he was then.

Still, I wish I could call him back, as Ray Kinsella calls back the players in *Field of Dreams*. I would love to ask him about the Albina

Tigers and Happy and Woozy. About his abusive father. I would like to tell him about how his grandson — me — and the two great-grandsons he never knew played second base, like him. And, finally, I would like to thank him for breaking the chains of abuse and for giving those of us who followed rose-colored hopes for the future.

Big leagues

In most parents' life, a time comes when their child finds himself thrust into the real world, girded for battle by years of parental guidance, ready to test his or her skills amid the turbulence of an ever-changing world.

It's called tee-ball.

Here's the journal of my youngest son's first season, during which he started on a team called the Pilots. He was 5:

April 30. Across town, the Seattle Mariners' motto this year is "Anything Can Happen." They picked the wrong team. Do Mariners players ever pretend their gloves are Halloween masks? The Pilots do. Have the Mariners ever gone two weeks without making an out? The Pilots have.

This is a team full of imagination, spunk and candor. Unfortunately, the only out the Pilots made today was when a grounder caromed off the second baseman's right ankle and accidentally rolled in the glove of the first baseman. Indeed, anything can happen — and does.

"Good job out in the field," one mom said to her son-the-center-fielder as the Pilots readied to bat. "Next time, remember your mitt."

With 18 kids on the team and a coach who looked like he'd rather be on a highway litter patrol, there wasn't much action today. In 75 minutes, my kid took two swings at the ball and fielded one grounder. I brought my movie camera. I should have used time-lapse photography.

May 7. The season has hardly begun and already the team has been racked by controversy. Apparently the Pilots' coach went off and got married, and his honeymoon went into extra innings. He's gone.

"Who cares about the coach?" says one mom. "My kid just wants his uniform."

The Pilots got their uniforms, but not my kid. In a surprise move that rocked the sports world, he was traded to the Cougars, an expansion team. There was no press conference. Nobody speculated about the terms of the agreement. Instead, the coach just said, "You, you, you and you — come with me." They ought to try that in the major leagues. It would be much simpler than the drawn-out contract negotiations.

The Cougars are a lot like the Pilots in that their outfielders sometimes play with their backs to the plate, and their infielders get easily distracted, say if someone in the stands blinks. When a ball comes their general direction, however, all 13 of them pounce on it like seagulls on crab bait. One kid fielded a grounder and tried to throw it to first. A teammate jumped up and blocked it.

So far, the biggest challenge for these kids seems to be making the transition from batting to going out in the field. When the two teams switch positions, it's like the changing of tides — it takes about half an hour and there's an undercurrent of confusion.

But the fans love it. One mother was so engrossed in the game she spent two innings reading a *National Enquirer* that included an article about a horse that can drive a 1960 Lincoln Continental. For a while that peeved me. But later, after the paper blew my way and I took a look at the article, I understood her fascination. Butterscotch — that's the name of the horse — can even honk the horn!

May 14. Depending on who you talk to, the Cougars either won 21-3 today or lost 17-5. I couldn't figure it out. One of the coaches actually tries to keep a scorebook on these games, a job slightly more difficult than charting the daily movement of all the salmon in Puget

Sound.

How, for example, do you score a play in which all three right-fielders muff a grounder, one of them finally throws it to the first baseman, who tries to catch it with the back of his left ear since he's busy watching a hot-air balloon in a nearby parking lot; the left-fielder's dad tosses the ball back on the field to the shortstop, who throws it to the pitcher, who throws it to the catcher, who tags out a player at home — only to find it wasn't the kid who hit the ball in the first place but the next batter up?

May 21. I couldn't help but notice today the different "ready" positions the players use while playing in the field. The three most popular seem to be:

• The Mitt Face. When the umpire yells "batter up," the defensive player puts his mitt over his face and peers through the finger gaps. This is perhaps the most versatile defensive position in that, besides preventing sunburn, it guards against dirt bombs being thrown by mischievous infielders.

• The Hand in Pocket. This position seems to work perfectly — until the player has a ball hit to him. Then, when his hand gets stuck, he's forced to throw opposite-handed or throw the ball with his mitt — always a favorite with the crowd.

• The About-Face. In what must be an apparent attempt to psyche out the batter, the infielder turns around and faces away from the plate. Not normally an effective way to scoop grounders, but great for balls that bounce off the legs of outfielders employing the Mitt Face or Hand-in-Pocket method.

June 4. What's the lost-ball penalty in baseball? The Cougars beat the Trail Blazers — or at least that's what all the Cougars said — in a game featuring exactly that. Maybe the stars were all aligned just right or the Cougars were all aligned just wrong or the outfield grass was a bit too long. Whatever, somehow a Trail Blazer batter hit a ground ball into the outfield that nobody on the Cougars ever saw. Finally, after getting directions from coaches and parents, the team found the missing ball in left-center.

June 11. The season ended today with a game against the Bombers. I must admit, there's been improvement. Those grenade throws of April have lost at least half their rainbow arc. Rarely do more than two runners find themselves on the same base at the same time anymore. I even noticed that the Cougars' shallow left-center-fielder — we have about a dozen outfielders — is remembering to wear his glove.

Not that there's not work to be done. Today's highlight came when one of the Bombers stole first base. I mean literally stole first base.

Turns out he was only using it as a Frisbee.

Homemade trophy

In 1989, professional golfer Mike Reid stood on the brink of winning one of the game's major championships — the PGA. He had a commanding advantage with only three holes left; like a stock-car racer with a huge lead, all he had to do was keep his car on the track for the final lap and the title was his.

But he couldn't. He bogeyed the last three holes and lost by a stroke. Reid was crushed. He flew home to Provo, Utah. There he was greeted by his family, including his oldest child, Brendalyn, then 8. She was holding something in her hand: it was, he realized, a homemade trophy. She handed it to him. On its side were inscribed these simple words: "No. 1 Dad."

Sometimes it's the innocence of a child that reminds us of the purest form of affection: Unconditional love.

Unconditional love is love that asks nothing in return. In a marriage, it doesn't require a prenuptial agreement. In a church, it doesn't require a tally sheet. In a parent-child relationship, it doesn't require an if-then clause.

It is love that demands nothing. Love with no strings attached. Love that perseveres despite the circumstances. It is also the most difficult love to give, particularly in the realm of sports, where so much is based on the very thing that unconditional love is not: performance.

I was keeping score at a fifth-grade basketball game when a mother rushed to me when it was over. She desperately had to know how many baskets her son had made. Curious, I asked why.

"We pay him 25 cents per point," she said.

I can understand an occasional financial reward for an outstanding report card. But intentional or not, what message — whether it's true or not — do we send to our children when we pay them per basket? Simple: that they are only worthy when they succeed. Never mind the more subtle message offered by the bucks-for-baskets approach — that the only thing valuable in basketball is scoring. (What, nothing for a solid game of defense? An unselfish assist so someone else might score? Great support from the bench?) What it really says is that there is a hidden tally sheet, there is an if-then clause, there are strings attached.

"Love," says 1 Corinthians 13, "is not self-seeking, it is not easily angered, it keeps no record of wrongs."

I'm a realist. I understand that in the business world, the person who sells the house gets the commission; I understand that the child with the high GPA and SAT scores gets the college scholarship. But in a time when children are aching for validation of their worth, we need to offer that validation based not on what they have done but on who they are — God's creations, worthy for their simply *being*, not their *doing*.

For parents, sports are a double-edged sword. We revel in our children's performances; what parent hasn't felt the pride of seeing his or her child score a goal or knock in a run or skate a strong routine? But we also can punish our children — if even through such subtleties as distancing ourselves from them after a game — when they've not met our expectations.

Only 10 weeks after he turned 18, my son, Ryan, won the men's club golf championship at the public course where he worked on the driving-range crew. He had chipped in for an eagle on the first sudden-death playoff hole against a former NCAA Division I player. I watched as he walked forward to receive his plaque in front of a group of guys mainly my own age. I was proud of him.

But two years later, that same son walked into our bedroom at 1 a.m. and, nearing tears, said, "I just wrecked my car." While reaching down to pick something off the floor, he had veered into a curb, wiped out two mailboxes, and done $1,800 worth of damage to a car that had cost only $1,500. Nobody was hurt. But I was not proud of him.

If, as a parent, I love my child more because he won that golf tournament and less because he wiped out a mailbox stand, my love is conditional.

"Love always protects, always trusts, always hopes, always perseveres," says 1 Corinthians 13:7. "Love never fails."

Yes, I believe parents should revel in their kids' successes. Better yet, we should revel in our kids, period.Once, my son, Jason, was on a summer baseball team that played about 50 games. One of his teammates, a pitcher, played in perhaps ten of those games — even then, perhaps for only an inning or two of relief. But his mother never missed a game.

That is unconditional love. That is a mother who's saying to her kid — even though he may not hear it until he's a parent himself: "I love you even when you're only keeping the pitching stats. I love you even if your ERA looks like a really good gymnastics scOregon I love you even when you give up a grand slam, miss a catcher's sign, walk the No. 9 batter. I love you even when your coach berates you or ignores you. I love you, period."

There's a difference between loving our kids at performance level and loving them at gut level. It's easy to support a kid when he's meeting our expectations; the challenge is supporting a kid when he's not.

It angers me when I see a coach in a youth game march to the mound, grab the ball out of the pitcher's hand and wave in a reliever — with disgust on his face. I'm not opposed to pitching changes; they're a necessary part of the game at that level. What I'm opposed to is the insensitive way they sometimes are made. No pat on the back. No "we-all-have-those-days" words of encouragement. No concern for a kid who already feels humiliated in front of his teammates and the crowd.

When a manger just grabs the ball and casts the pitcher aside, what that says to a kid is simply this: Your worth to me is totally dependent on your ability to throw a baseball. I care about you only for what you can do for me. Whatever affection I have for you can, in the time it takes to throw one wild pitch, disappear just like that — snap.

In essence, it says the opposite of 1 Corinthians 13. It says love is easily angered, it keeps a record of wrongs. It sometimes protects, sometimes trusts, sometimes hopes, sometimes perseveres; it all depends on the circumstances.

A while back, I noticed a familiar-looking young man, maybe 30 years old, at one of Jason's high school baseball practices. It was, I later realized, Todd Marinovich, a former NFL quarterback. A friend of his had once attended the same high school my son attends and, along with some other adults, they were engaged in a friendly game of home-run derby while players shagged balls in the outfield.

As I watched him take his cuts, I thought about this young man who once graced the cover of *Sports Illustrated* because of his football, not baseball, prowess. I've never seen a more tragic example of conditional love than the relationship Todd Marinovich had with his father.

Marv Marinovich, an ex-pro football player, brought up Todd with one goal in mind: to make him a superstar quarterback in the NFL. He conducted actual ball-tossing drills in his son's crib. He put his son on a regimented practice schedule as a pre-schooler. He brought in sports psychologists to work with Todd as a grade-schooler and a nutritionist who put Todd on a special diet.

Marv got the results he sought: Todd became a prep All-American, a freshman starter at Southern California, a No. 1 draft choice of the Oakland Raiders. But he later flunked out of the NFL, got involved in drugs and wound up in jail.

The tragedy is not that Todd couldn't cut it in the NFL; most of the planet's population couldn't cut it in the NFL. The tragedy is that he couldn't cut it with his father. The tragedy is that a father's demands cost the son his childhood. The tragedy is that after the great experiment failed, the father never saw the errors of his ways, never had the courage to begin anew with his son — in fact, began the same process with a younger son.

Sometimes those athletes with the most talent are the ones most susceptible to conditional love. I think of a man I know — once one of the top high school tennis players in California — who could win a match, 6-0, 6-1 and his father's first words would be, "So, what happened in that last game?" Nothing was ever enough.

Our children will fail. We will fail. As parents, if we can accept that as an opening premise in our lives and in the lives of our children, we're halfway home in our quest to love our kids unconditionally.

That doesn't mean we shouldn't set high expectations and help our kids to achieve those expectations; the movie *October Sky*, in which a coal-mining father tries to ground his youngest son's dreams to build rockets, shows how expecting too little from our kids can hinder them, too. But the parent who doesn't allow his or her child to fail is the parent whose love for that kid always comes with a hidden agenda, a hidden agenda that may haunt that child into adulthood.

Likewise, the parent who pushes a child too hard isn't doing what's best for that child. Instead, that parent is supporting a selfish desire to live vicariously through the kid.

James 1:19 speaks of our need to be "quick to listen, slow to speak, and slow to become angry ... ." At times, that means understanding that our children might have interests that aren't our interests. Do we love them enough to support them — or is our love conditional, i.e., only available if our children pattern themselves after ourselves?

A few years ago, my youngest son began playing the bass guitar. I neither shouted for joy nor took a reciprocating saw to his amplifier; what I did, in retrospect, was simply try to tune out this new hobby. To pretend it wasn't actually pounding upstairs as I tried to write downstairs. To hope, like a nagging cold, it would just somehow go away.

One night, I'd been asked to speak to the youth group at our church and, before I was on, the youth band played. There, for the first time, I listened to my son play his bass guitar as part of a band. In a single moment, I saw the bigger picture. I saw all that I had been missing. I heard him, through music, praising the God of the universe and I thought: Wow. That's my kid.

I was humbled. I realized I had been just like that father in *October Sky* and had done nothing to encourage this interest of my son. After we were home, I told Jason that. I apologized. I told him I was proud of him. The next morning, I found a note in my briefcase from Jason, a guy who doesn't leave many notes.

It said I'd done a "great job" on my talk and that he was proud of me, a note whose subtle message was probably "Thank you so much for not embarrassing me like I thought you might." But I took that note and pinned it to my bulletin board because I had never had a note like that from him. What prompted it? My willingness to listen to him, appreciate him and share my feelings with him.

What it comes down to, I've realized, is loving others as God loves us: unconditionally. It's grace. It's making an allowance for others' shortcomings. It's loving our kids no more when they've made a game-winning hit, loving them no less when they've struck out and listening to them even when the bass music isn't our idea of a sweet sound.

It's a little girl presenting her father with a homemade trophy, not because of what he has done, but because of who he is: "No. 1 Dad."

And it's a father who, decades later, keeps that trophy in his display case, along with the other, less important, ones.

Breaking away

I was sitting in a bathtub full of moldy sheetrock when my then-13-year-old son, Ryan, asked the question.

"Can you take me golfing sometime?"

I had a bathroom to remodel. The forecast for the next week was for 150 percent chance of Oregon's liquid sunshine. I wanted to say no.

"Sure," I said. "What did you have in mind?"

"Well, maybe you could, like, pick up Jared and me after school on Friday and take us out to Oakway."

"Sounds good."

Friday came. The April showers continued. Looking out the window, moldy sheetrock seemed the saner choice. But at the appointed hour, I changed from home-improvement garb to rain-protection garb and loaded the boys' clubs and mine in the back of the car.

In front of the school, Ryan and Jared piled in. Ryan looked at me with a perplexed look on his face.

"What's with the golf hat, Dad?" he said.

It was, I thought, a silly question, like asking a scuba diver: *What's with the swim fins?*

"Well, I thought we were going to play some golf."

There was a peculiar pause.

"Uh, you're going, too, Dad?"

Suddenly, it struck me like a three-iron ripping my ego off the tee of fatherhood: I hadn't been invited. Thirteen years of parenting flashed before my eyes. The birth. The diapers. The late-night feedings. Helping with homework. Building forts. Fixing bikes. Cleaning up vomit. Going to games. Going camping. Going everywhere together — the two of us.

Now, I hadn't been invited. This was it. This was the end of our relationship as I'd always known it. This was adios, Old Man, thanks for the memories, but I'm old enough to swing my own clubs now so go back to your rocking chair and crossword puzzles.

All these memories sped by in about two seconds, leaving me about three seconds to respond before Ryan would get suspicious and think I had actually *expected* to be playing golf with him and his friend.

I had to say something. I wanted to say this: How could you do this to me? Throw me overboard like unused fish bait? We'd always been a team. This was Simon leaving Garfunkel right during the middle of "Parsley, Sage, Rosemary and Thyme." I needed to level with him. I needed to express how hurt I was. I, I —

"Hey, I'm up to my ears in that remodel project," I said. "Make some pars for me."

We drove on in silence for a few moments.

"So, how are you planning to pay for this?" I asked, my wounded ego reaching for the dagger.

"Uh, could you loan me $7?"

Fine, he doesn't want me, but he'll gladly take my money.

"No problem," I said.

I dropped him and Jared off, wished them luck and headed for home. My son was on his own now. Nobody there to tell him how to fade a 5-iron, how to play that tricky downhiller, how to hit the sand shot. And what if there's lightning? What about hypothermia? He's so small. Who would take care of him?

There I was, alone, driving away from him. Not just for now. Forever. This was it. The bond was broken.

I walked in the door. "What are you doing home?" my wife asked.

I knew it would sound like some 13-year-old who was the only one in the gang not to be invited to the slumber party, but maintaining my immature demure, I said it anyway.

"I wasn't *invited*."

There was another one of those peculiar pauses. Then my wife laughed. Out loud. At first I was hurt. Then, I too, laughed, the situation suddenly becoming so much clearer.

This is what fathers and sons must ultimately do. This is what I've been preparing him for since he first looked at me and screamed in terror: not to play golf without me but to take on the world without me. With his own set of clubs. His own strategy. His own faith.

I returned to the soggy sheetrock and remembered a time when I was about 13 years old. My family was camping and some family friends needed to be picked up three miles away, across the lake. My father looked at me. "Bob, would you like to take the boat over and get them?"

"Me? Alone?" I had never driven the boat alone before.

"Yes, you alone."

I drove the boat by myself that day — drove away from my father. Now, 25 years later, I drove away from my own son so that, even if in a suburbanized, '90s version of a father-son letting-go, I could allow him the rights of passage that my father had allowed me.

A few hours later, I heard him walk in the front door. I heard him complain to his mother that his putts wouldn't drop, that his drives were all slicing and that the course was like a lake. He sounded like someone I knew. Me. His tennis shoes squeeked with water as I heard him walk back to where I was working on the bathroom.

"Dad," he said, "my game stinks. Can you take me golfing sometime? I need some help."

I wanted to hug him. Rev my radial-arm saw in celebration. Shout: "I'm still needed!"

Instead, I got one of those serious-dad looks on my face and said, "Sure, Ry, anytime."

Do not go gentle

Do not go gentle into that good night.
Old age should burn and rave at close of day;
Rage, rage against the dying of the light.
— Dylan Thomas

I line up the six-foot putt. All is quiet, save for a few people talking quietly in the distance. Slowly, I take the putter back and stroke the ball. For a split second, the ball rolls toward the hole, then slides decidedly off to the right, like a car exiting a freeway long before its destination.

"Maybe you'd like to try something else," says the young salesman, watching from beside the artificial-turf putting green.

For an instant, our eyes meet. I am standing in one of the West Coast's largest golf shops and a young man 25 years my junior is telling me — behind his veneer of entrepreneurial etiquette — that I cannot putt.

After 32 years of golf frustration, it is time, I've decided, to face the reality that I can no longer blame my ineptness on my irons or woods. Instead, I've decided to blame it on my putter. So here I am, shopping for a new one. After nine years, I am kissing my Northwestern Tour model good-bye for a younger, sleeker model.

I feel so cheap; alas, I am a desperate man. At 45, my golf game is going through a mid-life crisis. And so it has come to this: a belief, a hope, a desperate clinging to the idea that I can somehow buy my way back to respectability.

Long a believer that the swing, not the equipment, makes the golfer, I've scoffed at friends who plunk down hundreds of dollars to find "new-and-improved" clubs to help them once again hit the drives of their youth. I've chided them for seeing some pro win a tournament, then rushing out to buy the replica of the putter he used; after Jack Nicklaus' stunning Masters win in 1986, who can forget that rush on those putters whose heads were roughly the size of bricks? The golfer makes the club, I've long insisted, not the other way around.

But in recent years, my game has gone so far south that even my putter talks with a twang. Blame it on a schedule where golf now makes only a rare guest appearance; after months of not playing, I usually prepare for a round like I prepare for a yearly dental checkup: by flossing the night before — i.e., hitting a bucket of balls, and hoping I can fool the hygienist. Of course, it never works — in the dental chair or on the golf course.

Blame it on a number of other excuses; the bottom line is that some saleskid who didn't even start shaving until after the invention of the Big Bertha driver is now trying to help save my golf game.

I look up at the kid with one of those don't-you-think-I-know-what-I-need looks on my face, then put my pride on a leash. "Sure, let's try something else."

"If you'd like, you can go out on our real putting green and test them," says the young salesman.

The kid is nice — he's only trying to help, after all — but something about this situation just doesn't seem right. I take three putters, a couple of balls and walk toward the outdoor putting green.

"Uh, I'll need you to leave your driver's license," he says.

I stop, a tad surprised. "I'll only be, like, 200 feet away," I say.

"Store policy."

You gotta be kidding. What's he think I'm going to do — take three putters and a couple of Titleists and hop the first flight to Mexico?

"Seriously?" I say, thinking that my slight balking will probably wave the mandate.

"Sorry."

I look at the young man incredulously and say the only thing that's left to say.

"But I'm your *father*. Doesn't that count for something?"

"Sorry, store policy."

I pull out my driver's license and hand it to the kid I once taught to drive. The kid I once taught to play golf. The kid I haven't beaten on a golf course since he was a sophomore in high school.

I love this kid. I'm proud that, at age 20, he's found himself a job that he likes and is good at. I think it's wonderful that he has developed into a near-scratch golfer who has shot 69, won back-to-back men's club championships and posted an 84 at night, using a glow-in-the-dark ball.

But deep inside I have this tiny dream: to beat him just one last time, at anything: golf, home-run derby or h-o-r-s-e on the backyard hoop. Like Nicklaus coming back to win the Masters at age 47, I'd like one last hurrah to remind the world I'm still around.

It's not a vindictive thing at all. It's just a little pride thing. Not a chest-beating thing, but Pride Lite. Father-son pride. It's wanting to be the hero one last time. It's wanting to still be considered significant, like when you give your son a bit of advice about life itself and he tries it and it works and you think: I'm still needed. I still matter.

And one more thing: Weird as this may sound, fathers want their sons' approval. In Ryan's journal, I wrote this about the first time we played golf together as a team. He was 16:

> Going to the 18th, the two teams were all even. I nailed a 152-yard 7-iron to within two feet of the cup, sunk the putt for birdie and we won! But I was so nervous standing over that putt, more nervous than you'll ever know. (Until now.) Why? Because I wanted so badly to prove to you that I wasn't just this hacker of a dad. That I could pull through. That I could produce under pressure. Because I want you to be the same kind of guy, whether the venue is golf, marriage, work, whatever. I want you to pull through when you need to. Withstand the pressure.

"Do you wanna try one of these putters?" he asks, snapping me back to reality. "This is like the putter you bought me when I beat you for the first time."

I remember the day. He was 15. I shot 88. He shot 86. Though I'd done all I could to prevent it, I was glad he'd won. Proud to have been outdueled by my own son. I wrote a mock newspaper article — *Ryan stuns Dad for first win!* — and made good on a promise to buy him the putter of his choice.

Since then, it's been his show; I've watched proudly from the edges of the fairway. And learned what it must be like for a kid to grow up with high-achieving parents because whenever I play now, people expect me to be good because Ryan is. And I'm not.

Not long after Ryan won his second men's club championship at a Eugene public course, I teed up my opening drive at the same place and promptly hit it out of bounds. It was like Einstein's father flunking Algebra I.

"So," said the starter, "you're Ryan Welch's father, huh?" As if he really wanted to say, "So much for that axiom about the acorn not falling far from the tree, huh?"

For the most part, I've accepted this role reversal. Twice now, Ryan has had me caddie for him in tournaments that brought together all the winners of club championships from around the state. And I've considered it one of the highest honors a father could be accorded: to be able to carry on my back the clubs of a son I used to carry in my arms.

But deep down, the instinct quietly gnaws at me to prove myself — to nobody else but myself.

That instinct welled up one Fourth of July. A bunch of families had gathered at the home of our friends the Schars, whose large front yard and the growing twilight begged for a game of Wiffle ball.

Naturally, two teams were divided: Youth vs. Old Codgers Who Can't Even Change a Light Bulb Without Being Sore the Next Morning. It was humiliating. The punks were hitting balls so high the FAA was probably picking them up on radar. Our outfielders were forced to play so deep we were in a small orchard, next to a barn.

Then came the True Moment. It was, we had decided, the final inning. Two outs. I was playing right field and Ryan was at bat. He drilled a hot grounder my way. I made the stop and instinctively readied to fire it to second, then realized Ryan was nearly already there.

In a split second, I realized what was happening: He had no intention of stopping. He was going full bore, intent on stretching a routine single into a home run. He was doing what 20-year-olds instinctively do when competing against their fathers in front of a crowd of people, including their girlfriends: trying to humiliate their fathers with an in-your-face touch of arrogance that I would have done myself 25 years ago.

I could have thrown the ball to third base and hoped for the best, but Wiffle balls, sometimes with even a breath of wind, can sail away like Sky King's plane at the start of his old TV show, just as the announcer says "Brought to you by Nabisco!" What's more, in games like this, the team at bat provides the catcher, and so it's not uncommon that they "accidentally" drop the ball when trying to make the tag or "accidentally" sprain an ankle just before the ball arrives.

I knew what had to be done. As Ryan neared second, I locked my eyes on home plate — actually, home rag — and, ball in hand, headed for it like a bird dog on a bead. I was going to single-handedly make this out.

My teammates would think I was crazy; the play called for a throw to second or third. But they didn't know my son. They didn't know me — the deep, mid-life me. True, this was Wiffle ball, not golf. But at age 45, you take your opportunities where you can find them. This was my Don Quixote moment to dream the impossible dream … to fight the unbeatable foe … to right the unrightable wrong, i.e., that youth should somehow get the last laugh.

About the time I crossed the base path between first and second, Ry was swinging wide around third base and hot-dogging his way home in front of the two dozen spectators.

We were two generations on a collision course, the Road Runner and Wily Coyote with plans to outfox one another; father and son on missions for the ages.

At the pitcher's mound, I felt my first sense of hopelessness. He was too young, too fast, too committed to succeed — and only about 15 feet from reaching that success. But in every athlete's mind there comes a split-second when you must decide whether you will absolutely lay yourself flat to win or give something less. In that split-second, I didn't care if this was just a pick-up game at a Fourth of July picnic; I was going for it.

I tilted forward like a sprinter preparing to break the tape — perhaps too far forward. I started to stumble and lose control, my feet unable to keep pace with my desire and ego. Had I been an F-15 trying to land on the USS Teddy Roosevelt, the air boss on the radio would have been screaming: "Pull up! Pull up! You're coming in too hot. Pull up!"

But it was too late. I was either going to tag this kid an instant before he touched home rag or crash and burn trying. For the first time, Ryan glanced left and realized he wasn't trying to beat the ball home, but his father carrying that ball. Momentarily, he eased up, as if to suggest he was going to hammer home this humiliation like one of those oh-so-cool football players who, moments before hitting the end zone for a certain touchdown, slows down to mock the defender.

Then, when he realized I actually had a chance to make the play, his eyes filled with fear, like a horse spooked by a rattlesnake.

Six feet from the rag, Ryan dove with all he had. Six feet from the rag, I dove with all I had. I reached out in mid-air and strained to touch the ball to his back just inches before his hand reached home. We both went sprawling, Ryan heading south, me heading south-southwest. No umpire was around to yell "safe" or "out" but everybody knew the truth: I had nailed him. The kid was out.

Fans and players alike whooped and hollered. The two of us got up, a crazed man who still thought of himself as a boy and a wild boy who thought of himself as a man. Both of us drenched in sweat. Both of us huffing and puffing — one of us a bit more than the other.

Our eyes met. He gave me a small nod, then a hand slap. Though he'd done all he could to prevent it, he seemed somewhat proud that I had won this dual of the decades. Proud that his father had the gumption to beat the odds. And him.

Weeks later, at the golf shop, I returned from the practice putting green to where that same young salesman was waiting.

"I'll take this one," I said, showing him the putter I had chosen.

He handed me back my driver's license, then started waxing poetic about some kind of Big Bertha 3-wood. I had no intention of buying a 3-wood; equipment is overrated. The golfer makes the club; not the other way around. But by the time I walked out of the store half an hour later, I'd not only bought the putter and that 3-wood, but a 5-wood as well. (What can I say? The kid is a good salesman.)

We said good-bye. Ry headed off to help another customer, to continue his quest of making his own way in the world. New clubs in hand, I headed off to the driving range, to rage against the dying of the light.

Seasons to come

It had been Ryan's first major league baseball game, and as we walked away from Seattle's Kingdome, I was lost in thoughts of my grandfather playing baseball in 1905, the nostalgia of the game, the way sports can bind together a father and son like the lacing of a well-made mitt.

"Ryan," I said to the 4-year-old kid, "what was your favorite part of all that you saw tonight?"

After an evening of hot dogs and home runs, of souvenirs and singing "Take Me Out to the Ball Game," after talking baseball strategy and doing the Wave, it soon became clear that what had impressed Ryan most was none of this stuff. It wasn't the color guard that performed the national anthem. It wasn't who won the game. It wasn't even the design of the teams' uniforms or the computerized scoreboard.

It was the 60-foot-long men's urinal.

"How can it be so long?" he asked.

That was 1983. Two years later, at age 3, his brother, Jason, would join us. I still have the photograph of him eating his first hot dog at a major-league baseball game. Not that a father would ever forget such a historic moment. You remember the first hot dog. You remember what impressed them about their first major-league game. You remember it all, the memories like logs on a winter's fire, there to keep you warm in the off-seasons.

It is now July 2006. Ryan and Jason and I are headed north on Interstate-5 to a Mariners-Red Sox game. The 31-year-old father who snapped the photo that night is now 52. Ryan is 27, married and the father of a 14-month-old son, Cade. Jason is 24 and will be married in less than two months.

This idea, in fact, was in honor of him, our baseball player. A sort of G-rated bachelor's party, the three of us once again going to a Mariners game as we had done often when living in the Seattle area in the '80s. As we drove north I did the math: it had been 17 years since we had last watched a Mariners game together, just the three of us.

Living in Eugene, it's now a five-hour drive for us. But it seems just like old times. And, well, nothing like old times. Instead of $8 for a reserved seat, for example, I've paid $50 apiece for three seats in the lower rightfield section. I've taken out a small equity loan to pay for a day's worth of food. Our tickets are no longer thin cardboard, but 8 1/2 by 11 sheets of copy paper I printed on my Epson printer after purchasing the seats online. And gone are the 60-foot-long men's urinals, replaced by individual units — and flanked by platforms on which to change baby diapers. (I can hear Tom Hanks now: *There's no diaper-changing in baseball.*)

But, let's face it, change can be good. The dreary Kingdome where we made those first memories — a virtual mausoleum with artificial turf — was imploded six years ago and replaced by Safeco Field, which is what a baseball park should look and feel like: brick and iron and personal, a place where fans are made to feel like a priority, not an afterthought.

And, on this day, we've been blessed with a sky above that's UCLA blue, not a given in often-cloudy Seattle. Instead of 15,000 people scattered around a Kingdome designed for football, a near-capacity crowd of 45,975 packs Safeco like multi-colored cake sprinkles. On this day, Safeco will outdraw Yankee Stadium; in fact, only one major-league ball park — the Mets' — will have a bigger turnout.

With a huge number of Boston diehards on hand, the game has an almost "football feel" to it, the visitors starting "Let's go, Red Sox!" chants and Mariners fans soon drowning them out. Between innings, seven infield-sweepers, as music pounds from the loudspeakers, suddenly segue into a well-choreographed dance, using their brooms as props. Fans are soaking up every pitch like sips of a cool lemonade on hot day, which this is.

The capper: simply the best major-league game the three of us have ever seen. Eight lead changes and ties. Seventeen runs. Seven doubles. And three home runs, one the first inside-the-park homer in Safeco history by Adrian Beltre in the bottom of the eighth to give Seattle an 8-7 lead; one a two-out blast to the deck above us by Boston's Jason Varitek to tie the game in the top of the ninth; and the grand finale: a walk-off blast to left-center by Seattle's Richie Sexson in the bottom of the ninth to win it, 9-8.

The crowd cheers and sings and claps and hoots and hollers for minutes after the game. Even those of us rooting for the Red Sox couldn't be bitter; it had been too good a game. I turned to some fan down the row. "Would you mind taking a picture of us?"

I knew Ryan and Jason might think it geeky. I didn't care. Someday I wanted to remember this day. Someday I wanted to show this photo to my grandson, Cade, and say: this was the best game your father and your uncle and I ever watched together.

As I drive home, Jason sleeps in back. Up front, Ryan looks west, to the lower reaches of Washington's Puget Sound, lost in thought. Meanwhile, I'm lost in mine. "Ever the sentimentalist," as a friend reminded me the other day, I find myself thinking back on this fatherhood journey: the good times, the not-so-good times, the changing times. The times when, even bathed in humor, you realized a certain disconnect beween you and your sons, times when you did something that caused your kids to roll their eyes and think: *Is there anyone on the planet less cool than my father?*

When Ryan was 16, we listened to an Oregon-Washington football game together on the radio in Eugene. After the game, he left for work at local golf course but I stayed and listened to a local radio station's call-in show. The University of Oregon fans were justifiably proud. But pride turned into gloating, and gloating into Husky bashing, and Husky bashing into individual-player bashing. In particular, the host and callers were razzing the Husky field goal kicker, who had missed two last-minute attempts to win the game.

They were sarcastically thanking him over the air. Saying he flat-out choked.Saying how glad they were that it wasn't them returning to his fraternity house that night.

Enough. Before I knew it, I had climbed on my moral high horse, cellular phone in hand, probably spurred on by some subliminal childhood message from my mother. When a team was getting blitzed to smithereens, she would always say something like: "Those players have mothers, too. I feel sorry for them."

"You're on the air," the host said.

I introduced myself, said I was thrilled to see the Ducks win, but thought that some of the callers had stooped too low in riddling the Husky kicker.

"Sorry, Larry," said the host, "but I disagree."

"It's Bob, not Larry."

"Whatever."

The host, apparently not a fan of 1 Peter 3:9 ("Do not repay evil with evil or insult with insult"), said Duck fans had a right to be obnoxious because Husky fans are obnoxious when Washington wins, which, as of late, had been most of the time.

"But," I said, thinking of a line I had used over the years with my youth teams, "we've got to win with class and lose with class. The stuff I've heard isn't very classy. What if that kicker were your —"

"Sorry, Larry Bob," said the host. "Got another caller. 'Bye."

Larry Bob? Just like that, the soapbox was pulled out from under me. But I shrugged it off and went on with my day. When Ryan got home from work that night, I asked if he had listened to the call-in show. He said he had, on his car radio while en route to his job at the golf driving range.

"Did anyone on there sound familiar?" I asked.

"Nope," he said and headed up the stairs.

Suddenly, on the fourth step, he froze. "Wait a minute. Hold on. Dad, that wasn't — I mean, no. Tell me that wasn't — you weren't that Larry Bob guy, were you?"

I started laughing.

"I don't believe it," he said, turning and burying his face in his hands. "We've just beaten the Huskies, everyone's enjoying the win and here comes this guy on the radio to spoil the party. And it turns out to be my own father!"

I laughed harder. He didn't laugh at all. OK, well maybe a little.

"Honestly," he said, "when I heard that guy, I said to myself: 'Get a life, buddy.' I'm like, 'I gotta tell Dad about this guy. He's a total loser!' "

Ninety minutes to go until we're back home. The sun has set, bathing Oregon's Willamette Valley in a defused pink. Even with the windows up, we can smell the fresh-cut grass fields.

By now, Jason is awake. And, ever the organizer, I suggest a game to keep us awake for the home stretch: each of us gets to ask one "big life" question to someone else. A pitch of his choice. No chin music, of course. But, hitters, no standing in the box with the bat on your shoulder, waiting for a fat one.

I ask Jason what drew him to Deena, his fiancee. And, like the kid who hit that stand-up double against the Oakridge pitcher, he clobbers it. Jason asks Ryan how, with his five-year wedding anniversary approaching, he's different now as a husband than he was in his first year. He takes it deep to the wall. And then I step into the box.

"If you could go back in time and do one thing differently as a father, what would it be?"

Oh, great. This game had been fun until now. Staring at the now-dark freeway in front of me, the windshield splattered with bugs, I want to hold up a single hand and step back. Timeout, ump. But, then, who was it who taught these guys the game?

Me.

"I would have been quicker to understand that the two of you were different, that you, Jason, weren't a clone of your older brother," I said. "After Ryan left for college, I think I expected you to be him. Ryan was a great golfer, and I thought you could be as good or better. But suddenly you were telling me you were going out for baseball. And I'm thinking: But you'll get eaten alive. You'll never even make the team. And yet you started on varsity late in your sophomore year. And made Midwestern League all-stars twice in a row."

Years later, when Jason announced, at 22, he was going out for a semipro football team, I cringed; the kid had never played a down of organized tackle football, was 5-foot-8 and would be playing against at least a sprinkling of players who had played Division I football. At season's end, he made the league all-star team and was voted his team's Most Valuable Player.

And I was reminded to not be so narrow-minded. To not assume, for example, that just because his brother hadn't played football didn't mean he couldn't.

So, yes, I would have realized that God doesn't make two of a kind. And that's not a bad thing. That's a good thing. Appreciate the uniqueness of each.

"Beyond that, I would have learned to ratchet back my expectations of you both," I said. "I think we should always shoot high and I don't think I was ever that push-push-push parent when it came to sports. But sometimes, say, in wanting our family to have the perfect experience, I think I could get more hung up on that expectation instead of just relaxing and enjoying the moment."

There was a pause. "But I want you to know that although I've expected much from you both, you've far exceeded whatever I'd hoped for." And we drove on in the dark.

Soon we arrived to drop Ryan off at his house. His wife, Susan, was reading. Their son, Cade, slept in his room.

I opened the door a crack and leaned over his crib. His pajamed rump jutted into the air like a '57 Chev whose chassis had been lowered in the front and raised in the rear. It had been a long time — more than two decades — since I'd seen a child sleeping like that.

I looked at that face. Such contentment. Such innocence. Such stillness for a little boy who, like his father and, I suppose, his grandfather, lives like a battery-operated toy with no "Off" switch.

Already, a Wiffle ball hangs by twine from our apple tree in the backyard of our house. (Don't look at me; it was the idea of Cade's grandmother, Sally.) The tree is near the first base line from the old BBA field where Cade's father and uncle played the Wiffle ball games as little boys and not far from the shed in which their Atlanta Braves and Monroe Middle School baseballcaps still hang, aged with tablesaw dust.

Already, Cade has learned to hit that hanging ball with a plastic bat, his swing a wild back-forth motion that looks more like he's trying to rip a pinata than connect with a baseball. But, oh, when he does connect, he'll sometimes smile as if, finding for the first few times, the joy of the game.

He and I share something in common: at 52, I aspire to play with the spirit of a 12-year-old. And so, of course, does he. We're just coming at that aspiration from different directions.

Maybe he'll grow up to be a chemist or guitar player or writer or teacher. Who knows? But as he grows up, I figure, he at least needs a chance to dream of hitting an Effie Ball, even if the woman for whom the home-run blast was named passed on years ago and the maple trees guarding her old house are far taller than they once were.

So, soon after the ball was hung from the tree, I went to the shed and got the Alumagoal All-Steel Dry Line Marker and filled it with lime chalk. Then, in the spirit of his great-great grandfather, Will Adams, and those who've followed, I did what I knew I must do:

Began to create Cade Welch's own field of dreams — for whatever seasons might lie ahead.

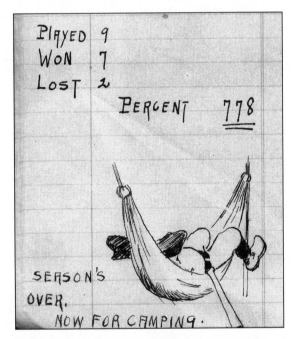

Will Adams' final sketch in his sandlot journal from 1905: "Season's over. Now for camping."

To contact the author, e-mail him at:
info@bobwelch.net.

For more information on Welch books
and speaking possibilities, see:
www.bobwelch.net

ALSO BY BOB WELCH

MY OREGON

The people, places and passion
through the eyes of a native son

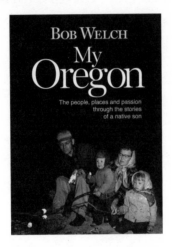

*" 'My Oregon' is Bob Welch at his finest. It is a
literary journey to the soul of a state,
reminding us that the virtues of a place
are found not only in trees and mountains
and beaches, but in people. Full of heart
and humor, this collection of essays belongs on
the shelf of everyone who calls Oregon home."*
— JANE KIRKPATRICK,
WINNER, 2005 DISTINGUISHED NORTHWEST WRITERS AWARD

AO Creative, Eugene, Oregon
Softcover $16.95
Available at bookstores and at www.bobwelch.net

ALSO BY BOB WELCH

AMERICAN NIGHTINGALE
The Story of Francis Slanger,
Forgotten heroine of Normandy

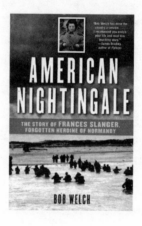

"A stirring story of intense personal devotion."
— PUBLISHERS WEEKLY

"Enrich your life and read this touching story."
— JAMES BRADLEY, AUTHOR OF FLAGS OF OUR FATHERS

"Has the golden cast of 'Saving Private Ryan'"
—BOOK BABES

"A heartwarming story for all ages."
—BOOKLIST

ALSO BY BOB WELCH

WHERE ROOTS GROW DEEP

Everyone leaves a legacy.
The only question is: what kind?

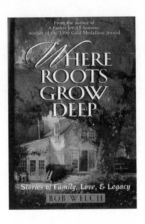

*"Makes us want to touch the world and change
the way we'll be remembered in it."*
— JANE KIRKPATRICK, AWARD-WINNING NOVELIST

*"Any reader will sense the rhythm of life as told
through simple yet profound stories."*
—THE HON. SEN. MARK. O. HATFIELD

"Filled with wisdom and hope."
—SANDRA ALDRICH, AUTHOR

Harvest House
Softcover $12.95
Available at www.bobwelch.net
or by e-mailing info@bobwelch.net

ALSO BY BOB WELCH

A Father for All Seasons

Stories of fathers, sons
and their journeys together through life

"A small jewel of a book."
— William Taaffe, Ex-Sports Illustrated editor

*"A tour de force of witty writing
and powerful storytelling."*
— The Bulletin, Bend, Oregon

*"Welch has done what only great writers
can do — unlock our own feelings."*
— John Fisher, author, musician

AO Creative
Softcover $12.95.
Available at www.bobwelch.net
or by e-mailing info@bobwelch.net

BOB WELCH AS A SPEAKER

*"Hands down, the most impressive speaker
we have heard in years. The response
was nothing short of remarkable."*
— ALEX RANKIN, ARCHIVIST,
BOSTON UNIVERSITY, BOSTON, MASS.

*"Stimulating, engaging, captivating ...
one of the highlights of the conference."*
— MIKE MONOHAN, EXECUTIVE DIRECTOR,
UNIFORMED NURSE PRACTITIONERS ASSOCIATION,
COLORADO SPRINGS, COLO.

*"There wasn't a dry eye in the room ...
one of the most inspiring and entertaining
events the medical society has sponsored."*
— CANDICE BARR, EXECUTIVE DIRECTOR,
LANE COUNTY MEDICAL SOCIETY,
EUGENE, OREGON

*"Totally consuming and uplifting.
Humorous. Great inspiration."*
— LYNN KRATER, CHAIR,
OKLAHOMA STATE COUNCIL OF PERIOPERATIVE NURSES,
STILLWATER, OKLA.

CONTACT INFO

Phone: 541-517-3936
Email: info@bobwelch.net
Web-site: www.bobwelch.net
Mail: P.O. Box 70785, Eugene, OR 97401